the world
of wine

Andrew Jefford

photography by Alan Williams

RYLAND
PETERS
& SMALL

LONDON NEW YORK

the world of wine
flavors and styles from grape to glass

For Grace Jefford and George Jefford

Senior Designer Louise Leffler
Editor Sue Morony
Indexer Hilary Bird
Production Meryl Silbert
Art Director Gabriella Le Grazie
Publishing Director Anne Ryland

First published in the United States
in 2000 as *Wine Tastes Wine Styles*
This edition published in 2006
by Ryland Peters & Small
519 Broadway, 5th Floor, New York, NY 10012
www.rylandpeters.com

10 9 8 7 6 5 4 3 2 1

Text © Andrew Jefford 2000, 2006
Design and photographs © Ryland Peters & Small 2000, 2006
Photographs on pages 14 center right, 16, 18, 32, 46,
57 below, 59, 60, 61, and 63 © Alan Williams

Printed in China

ISBN-10: 1-84597-236-8
ISBN-13: 978-1-84597-236-3

Library of Congress Cataloging-in-Publication Data

Jefford, Andrew.
    The world of wine : flavors and styles from grape to glass /
Andrew Jefford.-- 1st us ed.
            p. cm.
    Includes bibliographical references and index.
    ISBN-13: 978-1-84597-236-3
  1. Wine and wine making--Amateurs' manuals. 2. Wine tasting--
Amateurs' manuals. I. Title.
TP548.2.J44 2006
641.8'72--dc22
                                            2005034688

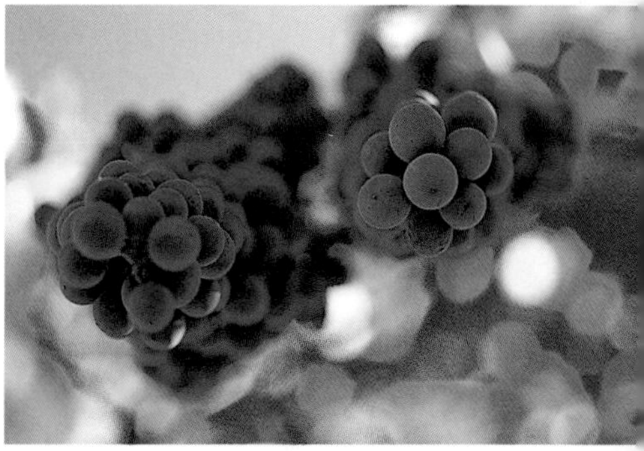

INTRODUCTION

DIONYSUS, SON OF ZEUS, DELIGHTS IN BANQUETS;

AND HIS DEAR LOVE IS PEACE, GIVER OF WEALTH,

SAVIOUR OF YOUNG MEN'S LIVES – A GODDESS RARE!

IN WINE, HIS GIFT THAT CHARMS ALL GRIEFS AWAY,

ALIKE BOTH RICH AND POOR MAY HAVE THEIR PART.

HIS ENEMY IS THE MAN WHO HAS NO CARE

TO PASS HIS YEARS IN HAPPINESS AND HEALTH,

HIS DAYS IN QUIET AND HIS NIGHTS IN JOY,

WATCHFUL TO KEEP ALOOF BOTH MIND AND HEART

FROM MEN WHOSE PRIDE CLAIMS MORE THAN MORTALS MAY.

THE LIFE THAT WINS THE POOR MAN'S COMMON VOICE,

HIS CREED, HIS PRACTICE – THIS SHALL BE MY CHOICE.

Euripides, *The Bacchae*, trans. Philip Vellacott (Penguin 1954, 1972)

Wine is the fermented juice of fresh grapes. There's a beauty about that plain definition, and a perfection of understatement.

Let's consider its beauty first. It lies in the emphasis on wine's simplicity. Every year, for example, in the quiet, hot, deeply incised Douro Valley in northern Portugal, a grape harvest takes place which closely replicates the thousands that have preceded it. During the day, high on the narrow terraces above the glassy river, grape pickers cut bunches from vines. Their voices echo in the still air. The younger men walk up and down the steep steps with baskets of grapes hoisted high on their shoulders. These are taken back to the *quinta*, or farmhouse, and emptied into large, shallow granite tanks. Towards nightfall, ten or twelve pickers, wearing shorts and T-shirts, climb into the tank and, linking arms, march to and fro across the mass of grapes. This slowly turns into a viscous, pippy gruel. After more treading, after dancing, after brandy and music and laughter, the must is left alone in the stillness of the night. There are yeasts in the air; fermentation begins. Grapes, foot-treading, air: wine is simple. Even under less picturesque conditions, wine very nearly makes itself.

And the understatement? That requires a little more explanation. Most of us enjoy, from time to time, the process of gazing back into history – initially, in personal terms: who were they, our progenitors? The further back we go, of course, the greater our genetic dissolution:

four grandparents swiftly multiply into the 2,000 or so direct ancestors of the 12th generation, 300 years back. Personal threads, thus, are swiftly lost, but it's entirely possible that I (for example) am the fractional descendant of a man or woman who, like Samuel Pepys or James Boswell, drank red Bordeaux and port in the taverns of a smaller and muddier London town than today's great and still wine-hungry city.

Culturally, we can look backwards around 6,000 years and still recognize ourselves, more nimbly waisted and almond-eyed, in the wall paintings of Egyptian tombs, or find dramas identical to those we live out today portrayed, with glittering economy, in the surviving books of Homer. Beyond these landmarks, the focus once again is lost. Yet even there, in the snapshots of human infancy, wine looms large as friend to man. Egyptian cup-bearers brought wine to drinkers who sat beneath the shade of vine arbors; when Homer's home-bound hero is welcomed by Alcinous, Circe and all those who give him shelter from the waves, the first thing they offer, alongside restorative meat, is "mellow wine". Indeed, Maron gives Odysseus no fewer than a dozen jars of a "red and honeyed vintage" so good he had kept it secret (as you or I might do) from his entire household, and it is this "dark wine" which Odysseus uses in defeating the cannibal giant, Cyclops. We may no longer consult with gods in columns of mist, nor seal up the carefully wrapped bodies of our rulers in gilded cells for eternity, but we still refresh our tired limbs and console our minds with the same pressed, fermented grape juice. Wine has long been with us.

Wine, too, has a meaningfulness no other drink possesses – save, perhaps, water itself. The sharing of wine and food with others is a fundamental gesture of hospitality. Keeping a cellar of wines is a way of capturing and hoarding warmth so that it can be released in little flurries when it is most needed. A bottle of wine is a kind of battery, charged with sunshine, flavor and memory. Among enthusiasts, wine tends to command affection, loyalty and commitment quite unlike that inspired by other drinks; and wine offers the intricacy and complexity which makes connoisseurship so richly possible.

Above all, wine carries a powerful symbolic charge. The ancient Greeks, argued one of their greatest 19th-century scholars, Friedrich Nietzsche, were driven by two forces. One was the Apollonian, water drinker's force of reason and balance, convention and law; the other was the dangerous and subversive Dionysian force of passion, inspiration and imagination. Dionysus was the god of wine. Nietzsche's vision was derived in part from *The Bacchae* of Euripides, in which wine is the symbolic key which unlocks a terrible yet necessary, liberating and finally refreshing part of human experience.

Within the Christian tradition, too, wine plays a key role, symboliz-

A bottle of wine is a kind of **battery**,

ing the blood of Christ within the Eucharist. No one brought up within societies in which Christianity is the dominant religious force can ever sip a glass of wine and not feel spiritually as well as physically recharged by the act, even if such feelings are so muted as to be unconscious. Few drinks have wine's ability to bolster resolve and salvage hope in hopeless hours, too: perhaps this is down to the beneficial minutiae of its chemical components, but it seems just as likely to be the symbolic husk it carries.

Wine's roots penetrate deep into the clay of history, then, and our long and loving relationship with it has lent it a potent symbolic force. However, another way in which wine matters deeply to us is its ability to link us to the world itself. Wine gives us a relationship to the world no other food or drink can. It permits us to taste the world. We'll explore this fully in the "Places" section of this book (see pages 36-69), but the principle is simple enough.

No two wines ever taste the same. Some wines, admittedly, are only weakly characterful and thus resemble each other by default, yet even in these wines there is usually a fundamental difference in the basic weight or shape of the wine in the mouth, or in the general flavor it suggests. Certainly, all good wines are palpably different from each other, and a major factor governing those differences is the earth in which the vines themselves are rooted. Grow Chardonnay in the Napa Valley, and it will taste markedly different from Chardonnay grown in the Loire Valley. The California wine will be richly constituted, high in alcohol and unctuous in texture; the French wine will be slender, clean, fresh but rather neutral in style. Indeed, in the very best wine-growing areas, differences of much greater subtlety than this can be discerned. In Burgundy, Chardonnay grown in three or four places on a hill, separated by a matter of yards, can vary to an extraordinary degree. Wine from a low or a high spot may be simple and straightforward, capable of aging for four or five years into a gently expressive, faintly nutty white. Wine from the middle of the hill, by contrast, may need at least ten years' aging before it opens up at all. When it does so, it will provide (over a 30-year lifetime) such depth and allusiveness of both

charged with sunshine, flavor and memory.

aroma and flavor that it will astonish all who drink it. These two wines might even be made by the same man or woman in an identical manner; the difference is, of course, the earth.

There is no other substance we can eat or drink which performs in that way. Other agricultural products are merely themselves, no matter where they are grown. Where there are flavor differences between, say, potatoes or carrots or corn, they are generally the result of a particular strain or variety, or the generosity of a season. Only grapevines can give a sensual print to a hillside, to a valley, to a region. Only vines can lend a scent and a flavor to geography itself.

Where are we in the history of wine? That is gloriously uncertain. The wine world of today is very differently constituted from 30 years ago; new changes and developments will certainly unravel over the next three decades. Wine's fundamental healthfulness, if enjoyed in moderation, is medically proven, and seems certain to increase global demand in non-wine-producing cultures. There is already a bewildering variety of wines available to us, which is yet another reason why defining wine simply as "the fermented juice of fresh grapes" is so perfect an understatement; we will have still more wines from which to choose in the future. Faced with this multiplicity of names, vintages and origins, how do we best learn about wine?

The approach of this book is threefold. In the first section, "The Taste of Wine", we will explore the three main routes to discovering wine for yourself: by grape variety, by learning about the places in which wine is grown, and by understanding winemaking strategies and the flavor impact of these. In the second section, "Wine Styles", we will explore wines themselves in the way in which most people buy and enjoy them – by style, in other words. Taken together, these two parts of the book will furnish both an understanding and a basic knowledge of wine. The third section, "The Pleasure of Wine", provides some hints on how to enjoy wine to the full. Then, of course, it's up to you.

When I first began to discover wine almost 20 years ago, I took a job in a wine shop. I remember being told that the only way to learn about wine was to taste it. The advice was sound enough, though my employer gave me all too few opportunities to follow it. Tasting *is* the only way to learn – and I am still learning. Don't worry about the names, the vintages, the facts and figures: there are reference books aplenty to take care of these. Concentrate, instead, on what really matters: the taste of wine. In doing so, you will connect with our earliest ancestors, both known and unknown; you will enjoy one of the earth's most expressive gifts; and you will help, by your passionate patronage, to create a still greater legacy of pleasure for future generations.

I remember it well: the delicious vertigo brought on by a slow browse around the tightly packed shelves of a wine shop. Every bottle intrigued; yet I knew that some would be more to my taste than others, while a few would be frankly disappointing and a waste of hard-earned money. Even now, after more than a decade spent writing about wine, I'm still far from able to declare with any confidence what every wine in a well-stocked store will taste like. But there are three routes by which I can, with some accuracy, narrow the field. So can you.

the taste of wine

The easiest way to anticipate the style of a wine is to learn what certain grape varieties taste like. Many wines, particularly those produced in countries like Australia, New Zealand, the US or Chile, are labeled according to the grape variety from which they are made. There are, admittedly, thousands of different grapes grown around the world, but most wines are made from one or two of just a dozen or so major varieties. If you familiarize yourself with the taste of these, you'll be able to predict with some accuracy the taste of most wines. Grapes, then, are the first route to identifying wine flavors.

Route One:
Grapes

CHARDONNAY

Everybody knows this white grape, and most drinkers love it. Indeed, it's so popular, wine-shop workers tell me, that occasionally customers ask for red Chardonnay, reasoning that it must be just as good as the white. (Sadly, it does not exist.) It is also thought by many British wine-drinkers to be a region of Australia, so closely associated are the two in the drinking public's imagination.

Chardonnay is an agreeable and amenable grape whose home is in Burgundy (there is a village of this name in the Mâconnais), but which has traveled the world with unparalleled success, producing pleasant and sometimes distinguished wines almost everywhere it puts down roots. At home in Burgundy, it is responsible for some of the world's finest white wines. These are often inarticulate in youth, but given time they blossom and produce complex aromas of nuts

and butter, toast and cream, wild mushrooms and meadow flowers. Firmly structured and dry, they can also offer great richness, with a wide repertoire of tastes including lemon, melon, peach and apple – and, of course, the same creamy, nutty, buttery notes suggested by the wine's aromas.

Wherever wine is grown, Chardonnay will be planted, and in general it will give an "international" style characterized by soft, lemony fruit, occasionally with some creaminess (especially if it has been given extended contact with its yeast lees (sediment) during vinification and maturation), and often with the toasty-vanilla character of oak. Chardonnay loves oak, and winemakers around the world have discovered that fermenting and aging simple Chardonnay in oak barrels or in contact with oak staves or chips can replicate, comparatively swiftly, the

richness which classic white burgundy takes years to acquire. Sometimes this is overdone, and such Chardonnays taste obvious and confected.

Burgundy itself has at least three classic styles, ranging from sour, mouthwatering, almost austere Chablis through the floral, structured grandeur of the great white burgundies of the Côte d'Or to the comparatively soft and honeyed comforts of Mâcon and its villages.

Other classic styles of Chardonnay include those of the finest Californian producers, which have a silkiness to them and great substance of flavor, combined with high alcohol levels, ripe, fruity character and complexity from contact with the wine's lees during and after barrel fermentation. Some regions (including Carneros and the Russian River Valley) produce tighter wines. Australia has several different styles ranging from the rich, pollen-scented, almost fiery Hunter Valley Chardonnays through the tapered elegance of Mornington Peninsula and Adelaide Hills examples. There is the piercing intensity of Tasmanian Chardonnay; lush, fat, creamy Barossa Valley versions; and finally the concentrated, poised, brightly defined wines of Margaret River. New Zealand's Chardonnays tend to be more slender and pithy, with pure, limey fruit; Chile and Argentina produce plenty of custard-rich

MAJOR WHITE GRAPES

Chardonnays (Argentina's often have grapefruit notes); while South Africa offers a variety of styles from the fresh, incisive Chardonnays of Elgin and Constantia to the richer versions of Stellenbosch and Robertson.

Like Cabernet Sauvignon, Chardonnay blends well with softer varieties of less pronounced personality; unlike Cabernet, though, the greatest Chardonnays are all unblended.

SAUVIGNON BLANC

This distinctive variety is responsible for some of the world's most easily recognizable white wines: grassy, fresh, zesty, crunchy, stony and made in the Upper Loire at Sancerre and Pouilly-Fumé. However, a consistent challenger recently for the Sauvignon Blanc crown has been New Zealand's Marlborough region, whose wines lack the flinty edge of the Loire examples, but make up for it with even more exuberant leafiness, green sap, gooseberry, asparagus and zingy lime.

Sauvignon Blanc's origins are in Bordeaux (it is one of the two parents of Cabernet Sauvignon) where, in combination with Sémillon, it produces its most subtle, soft and creamy dry whites in Graves and Pessac-Léognan. It is also blended with Sémillon to make the unctuous, amply oaked whites of Sauternes and Barsac. The creamy, dry, Graves style is that generally targeted by warmer wine-growing regions like much of California and Australia, yet with mixed success: such wines can lack freshness. South Africa produces crisp, elegant Sauvignon Blanc, especially in its cooler regions such as Constantia and the Darling Hills; so too can Chile, in Casablanca and San Antonio.

RIESLING

Some of the greatest wines in the world are produced from this peerless white grape. Because most of them come from Germany and none of them are oaked, this message struggles, salmon-like, against the torrents and cascades of fashion.

Riesling's attractions are threefold. First of all, it is an extraordinarily aromatic grape variety, and those aromas can reflect not only a range of fruits but also honey, minerals, flowers and (curiously, with age) gasoline. Secondly, its wines are nearly always finely balanced: the grape's slow ripening and the cool latitudes in which it is generally grown yield musts generously endowed with both sugar and acid. Traditional German vinification techniques are designed to emphasize this balance by retaining some residual sugar and arresting fermentation at relatively low alcohol levels. Thirdly, Riesling ages superbly: great German Rieslings can spellbind at 20 years old despite meager alcohol levels of just eight or nine percent alcohol by volume (abv); many more expensive and illustrious white burgundies of the same vintage will, by then, be dead and gone.

The biggest spectrum of Riesling wines comes from Germany and ranges from the taut, piercing styles of the Saar or Ruwer to the rich, spicy, unctuous wines of the Pfalz. Alsace Rieslings tend to be dry and severe, needing age before they soften and open out, but (as in Germany) this grape's potential for expressing mineral depths is remarkably realized in Alsace's Grand Cru examples. Riesling is also planted throughout the wine-producing countries of the southern hemisphere. The most successful results come, surprisingly enough, from Australia, whose warmer climates give wines utterly different in character to those found in northern Europe: they are ripe, full and sometimes domineering in character, with lots of mango, guava and citric notes. These robust, exuberant Rieslings partner summer foods very well.

SEMILLON

An increasingly popular white grape variety producing richly constituted dry and sweet wines in Bordeaux and parts of the New World, most notably Australia. In Bordeaux, Sémillon is usually blended with Sauvignon Blanc and often Muscadelle; these other varieties add fruit and freshness to its sometimes lumbering corpulence.

Some of the world's **greatest wines** are produced from this **peerless** white grape RIESLING

The results, especially when barrel-fermented, are complex, creamy and rewarding. For the sweet wines of Sauternes and Barsac, Sémillon's weight and syrupy texture is a luscious benefit, especially given the complex flavors derived from botrytis (see page 45). In Australia, and most famously in New South Wales' Hunter Valley, Sémillon makes varietal wines which, with age, acquire complex scents (cheese, lima beans, lime pith and toast) without ever quite matching those aromas with flavors of equal intricacy. The variety is often, though rather unexcitingly, blended with Chardonnay. Other countries' experiments with Sémillon have failed to produce wines with much character.

CHENIN BLANC

This variety is something of a chameleon. At its best, in the central part of France's Loire Valley, it can produce wines of extraordinary intensity and grandeur, with aromas and flavors hinting at wax, damp hay, pepper or honey, and in fruit terms at apples, grapes and apricots. Such wines can be dry

(for example, Savennières, Jasnières or Vouvray Sec), semi-sweet (Vouvray or Montlouis Demi-Sec) or sweet, with or without the benefit of botrytis (Vouvray Moelleux, Bonnezeaux or Quarts de Chaume). Great Chenin Blanc, however, needs a long growing season and careful vinification; when it doesn't get these, the wines can be acidic and coarse. The Loire trick is to use less successful Chenin for sparkling wines, which may make economic sense but is not the best way to succeed in quality terms: these *crémant* or *mousseux* wines can be steely and charmless.

Huge amounts of Chenin Blanc are grown in California's Central Valley and (as Steen) in South Africa. High yields under a hot sun deprive most of these wines of any interest, though they are good at keeping their acidity levels up under such circumstances. In South Africa, old bush-vine Chenin is beginning to be taken more seriously, producing wines of chewy intrigue, though its lightly tropical range of fruit flavors is quite different from the orchard fruits of Chenin made in the Loire Valley.

Other important white grapes

ALIGOTE

An amenable if unexciting grape grown in Burgundy, where it produces wines with greater acidic edge and incision and less buttery richness than Chardonnay. If you want to make a classic *Kir* (white wine poured onto a dash of crème de cassis), Aligoté is the traditional wine to use. This grape is also widely grown in Bulgaria and Romania, where it produces (at best) a fresh, easy-drinking white. It is occasionally blended with Chardonnay there.

COLOMBARD

This handy variety is widely planted in southwest France for distilling into Cognac and Armagnac and, when coolly and

carefully vinified, producing light, young, simple wines of crisp, grassy freshness in the Côtes de Gascogne. It is also extensively grown in California and South Africa to make off-dry to sweetish cheap whites.

GEWURZTRAMINER

Extraordinary pink-skinned variety grown in Germany, Austria, Alpine Italy and Eastern Europe, but never with as much success as in the region with which it is most closely identified: France's Alsace. There, in sunny sites, it produces rich, heady, almost oily, golden-white wines trembling with spice and rose scents and tasting of litchi nuts and ginger. Gewürztraminer usually has lowish acidity levels which can give less successful wines an impression of aimless bulkiness; the best, by contrast, are succulent, tight-knit and limitlessly rich. Southern hemisphere examples (from, say, Chile or New Zealand) can often be impressively spicy and show improving depth of flavor, too.

GRUNER VELTLINER

Austria's almost universally planted white grape does not produce, by international standards, notably characterful white wines, yet their sappy, peppery, food-friendly amenability makes them much loved, especially as heady, milky new wines sold domestically at wine stalls before Christmas. The variety, consequently, still occupies around a third of Austria's vineyards. Chewy depth, structure and complexity is possible in wines made from some fine sites in the Wachau region of the country.

MARSANNE

This rich variety from the northern Rhône produces fat, syrupy, low-acid wines, seemingly scented on occasion (as in the best Hermitage Blanc, for which Marsanne is combined with the more elegant Roussanne) with haunting meadow blossoms and flavored with white almond. It takes well to oak, and is increasingly planted as a vin de pays varietal across southern France. There are old-vine plantings of Marsanne in Australia's Victoria, too, producing unsubtle but memorably rich, heavy, dry whites packed with high-volume mango and apricot flavors.

MELON DE BOURGOGNE

Despite its bizarre name (which accurately betrays its Burgundian origins), this is the grape that produces Muscadet in the Loire region of France. It's almost completely neutral in aroma and flavor, but lees-aging (*sur lie*) gives appealing

hints of crisp lemon and yeast in young, fresh bottles.

MULLER-THURGAU
(Rivaner)

Widely grown but generally unexciting cross of Riesling and Madeleine Royal, much used in cheap, sweetish German blends. It is at its best in cool climates, like those of Luxemburg or England, where it can produce sometimes crisp, sometimes medium-dry white wines.

MUSCAT

An enormous family of vines, of which the two best are the Muscat Blanc à Petits Grains and Muscat of Alexandria; Muscat Ottonel is a coarser cousin. All share, however, the capacity to make wines which taste distinctly grapey. Muscat is sometimes fermented fully to give a light, musky yet dry wine – the ideal aperitif. In Italy, meanwhile, it is used to make sweet, refreshing, low-alcohol foaming wines such as Moscato d'Asti. In the main, however,

this variety is used for succulent, often fortified, sweet white wines, pungent with grape and orange scents and flavors. Long barrel-aging and deliberate oxidation can bring complexity and stylistic diversity to this fundamentally simple though grand and unmistakable grape.

PINOT BLANC
(Pinot Bianco)

Pleasant, easygoing variety yielding gently rounded, grape-scented white wines. The best and weightiest of these are found in Alsace and Austria (where late-harvest examples are sometimes used to make luscious dessert wines). More slender examples are common in Germany and Italy.

PINOT GRIS
(Pinot Grigio)

A white half-sister of Pinot Noir, widely grown in Alsace, Germany, Austria, Italy and Eastern Europe; New World plantings are on the increase, too, especially in Oregon. Once again,

however, Alsace provides the most inspiring model; its wines (sometimes also labeled Tokay d'Alsace) range from richly constituted, low-acid, full-bodied dry whites with aromas and flavors of spice, smoke and even bacon, to sweet, luscious, close-textured, pastry-rich, late-harvest wines. In Italy (as Pinot Grigio), it tends to produce a less rich style whose sappy depth partners food well.

ROUSSANNE

Intriguing, fragrant variety used with fat, low-acid Marsanne to make classic northern Rhône whites such as Hermitage, Crozes-Hermitage and white Châteauneuf-du-Pape; now being grown across the Languedoc for worthwhile vin de pays wines with a haunting, delicately peachy flavor.

SCHEUREBE

An interesting German cross of Silvaner and Riesling producing exotic wines with aromas and flavors including roses and mulberries. The Scheurebe grape produces high sugar levels but retains its soft acidity well, and is easily affected by botrytis.

SILVANER (Sylvaner)

Historically important vine much used across Alsace, Germany and central Europe. Its wines are light in character but sound, often dry, sometimes with hints of vanilla or pepper and with a soft, inarticulate earthiness.

TORRONTES

Unusual variety producing spicy yet dry, crisp, refreshing whites in Argentina, often with heady alcohol levels.

VIOGNIER

The northern Rhône Valley is the home of this aromatic, low-yielding variety and Condrieu is its flagship appellation. Indeed, the best Condrieu has proved so inspirational that plantings are increasing swiftly across the Languedoc and throughout California and Australia. Its attraction lies in the grape's rich scents – good Condrieu smells intriguingly like exotic flowers (freesia, jasmine, oleander, gardenia). Its fruit is less obvious (ripe peach or apricot); its texture deliciously syrupy. Oak is unnecessary; it is extravagant enough without. Most varietal Viogniers have not yet attained the extraordinary richness of Condrieu, but that is the aim.

MAJOR RED GRAPES

CABERNET SAUVIGNON

This grape provides the world's reference reds: structured, authoritative and long-lived. Like Chardonnay (but unlike either Pinot Noir or Merlot), Cabernet Sauvignon travels easily, managing as it does so to keep its personality intact. It is also an exceptionally good mixer, combining well with a range of varieties from Shiraz to Tempranillo. Moreover, few red grapes respond as well as Cabernet does to the influence of new-oak casks.

Back home in Bordeaux, and specifically in the Médoc and Graves regions, Cabernet Sauvignon is usually blended with Merlot, Cabernet Franc and a little Petit Verdot to make what, for many drinkers, is the archetypal red wine: a middleweight in maturity, with cedary, pencil-shaving scents and deftly layered flavors suggesting cassis, earth, tobacco leaf and dark chocolate. It reaches, in the finest wines of these districts, a peak of refinement and allusiveness which few other wines can match, and its life span after a good vintage will be 20 or 30 years.

Cabernet Sauvignon is grown wherever red grapes will ripen satisfactorily – including, of course, a number of other French regions. Some, like Bergerac and Buzet, produce wines not dissimilar to light Bordeaux; in the Languedoc, by contrast, it tends to express the ambitions (or lack of them) of its grower with wines which vary from deep, stern, and stony to frustratingly light.

Outside France, Cabernet Sauvignon is widely planted in Eastern Europe to create (at best) a range of throat-soothing reds based on an ideal of rounded, candy-like, mulberry fruit and (at worst) thin, green, weedy reds which have served time aimlessly in old, grubby wood. In Italy and Spain, however, it tends to be chosen by those who wish to make ambitious wines outside the confines of local traditions. The results can be impressive: deep

colors, subtly oaked scents and a rich mouthful of intense fruit/oak flavors, often backed by firm tannins. Cabernet's other European use is as a kind of discreet medicinal stiffener within traditional regional blends in areas like Spain's Navarra or Ribera del Duero, or Italy's Carmignano or Pomino. It is (misguidedly) permitted in Chianti Classico today.

Across the New World, everyone is serious about Cabernet Sauvignon. For sheer volume of flavor, California's ambitious growers produce the most explosive Cabernets of all: enormously tannic and alcoholic, barely tamed by oak. Their primal grandeur is unique, and they have real aging potential, unfolding slowly towards a lush, chocolate softness. The least successful Californian Cabernets (which, generally speaking, means the biggest brands) are merely affable, vaguely blackberry-toned, vaguely oaky reds.

For sheer drinkability at all levels, Chilean Cabernet is hard to beat. This is one of the most distinctive New World styles of all: its plum and mulberry fruit has a purity and exuberance no other country can match. Argentinian Cabernets can be good in a more thickly textured, earthy style.

Australia's most celebrated Cabernet-producing region is Coonawarra, a cigar-shaped strip of red soil over limestone situated in the cool far south of South Australia. At best, these wines offer bright fruit character and a startling intensity of flavor; French oak, integrated with customary Australian skill, is usually evident, too. Other great Australian Cabernet-producing areas include Margaret River (offering controlled power, dense flavors, slow evolution) and the Barossa and Eden valleys (rich, salty and full). Basic Australian Cabernet Sauvignon is generally blackberryish, though often needlessly acidic; the variety blends well with Shiraz.

New Zealand's Cabernets have not always been a great success; the variety is late-ripening and leafily vigorous, which means that in cooler climates like New Zealand's it can sometimes taste herbaceous and green (you'll find the same flavors in less successful Cabernets from Bulgaria and northern Italy). The best New Zealand Cabernets, though, are deeply colored and Bordeaux-like in a fresh-flavored way. Top South African Cabernet Sauvignon, again, offers clearly defined fruit flavor, generous tannins and a roasty warmth of flavor which bodes well for the future.

Since the greatest wines of the Médoc are world landmarks, blends of Cabernet Sauvignon with Merlot and Cabernet Franc are popular in most countries where Cabernet is grown. These are often among the finest reds of a particular region. Yet there is nothing sacred about that blend, and what is ideal for Bordeaux will not be ideal for every site around the world. In the long run, blends of Cabernet Sauvignon with other red grape varieties may prove more attractive than "the Bordeaux blend". What is certain is that Cabernet Sauvignon is a useful grape variety in mixtures: it adds structure, depth and seriousness to reds of softness and charm.

MERLOT

Merlot dominates Bordeaux's right bank, most celebratedly in St Emilion and Pomerol. The lushness and soft, sensual warmth of the best Pomerols and the aromatic meatiness of the best St Emilions have made them the darlings of the wine world. This, in turn, has sent Merlot racing around the new vineyards of both hemispheres as growers attempt to reproduce those winning characteristics – not, so far, with great success.

Merlot is Bordeaux's most widely planted variety since it occupies a substantial second place to Cabernet Sauvignon even in those areas, like the Médoc, where it is not dominant. It buds, flowers and ripens earlier than Cabernet, which is useful in Bordeaux where early autumn rain is the chief climatic hazard. The best Bordeaux Merlot is one of the richest reds in the world: full of creamy plum (St Emilion) or blackberry (Pomerol) fruit and, despite ample tannins, often silkily soft. It takes well to French oak, acquiring flavors of dark chocolate as it does so;

For **sheer drinkability** at all levels, Chilean Cabernet, with its pure plum and mulberry fruit, is hard to beat.
CABERNET SAUVIGNON

age brings a complex range of savory, meaty allusions.

Merlot is now widely grown in the south of France for vins de pays: these wines often hang on to the plummy fruit if nothing else. Italy's extensive Merlot plantations tend to yield simple, light reds, though serious, deep, carefully oaked examples are now emerging from Tuscany. It is also grown extensively in Switzerland and Eastern Europe to make enjoyable, juicy reds.

The most ambitious Merlots outside St Emilion and Pomerol are to be found in California. This, however, is a market-driven trend, rather than a choice the vineyards themselves dictate: Merlot in much of California is just too big, too alcoholic and too tannic, with dryish fruit. Sometimes this super-hunky style can be appealing, but it's a very different charm to the Bordelais original. Washington has only recentlydiscovered Merlot, but the dark, dense, chocolate-tinged results suggest that the variety might have more success there than further south.

Merlot in Chile has often been confused with Carmenère, but the clear stylistic fit between Chile's generally soft and comely reds and Merlot's own plummily supple profile looks set to provide some fine drinking in the future; Argentina, as usual, is offering more earthy, close-textured alternatives. South Africa and Australia run into some of the same heat problems with Merlot as California does, but cooler areas like Australia's Coonawarra are already producing Merlots of clearly defined, roundly spicy character, though these are sometimes over-acidified in the winery; the blend with Cabernet is usually a happy one. Generous vintages in New Zealand's warmer regions can create impressive Merlot in a brisk, fresh, minty style.

PINOT NOIR

"Capricious" is the word customarily tethered to this red variety, the grape which makes red burgundy. Pinot Noir is also grown in Champagne, Alsace and the Loire Valley; it produces many of the best red wines of Germany and Switzerland. It is also grown in almost every other wine-producing country of the world as the red grape of choice for cool-climate regions, for use in sparkling-wine blends, or quite simply because the producer loves great red burgundy and wants to echo some of those resonant flavors in his own vineyard.

Most red wines based on Pinot Noir have a light to medium depth of color, a delicate tannin structure but relatively prominent acidity. At its best, Pinot Noir produces wines of seductive, arresting perfume (cherries and raspberries in youth, and more complex, gamey notes with age); thrillingly vivid, searching flavors, and textures which soften relatively swiftly to a silky maturity. Great red burgundy seems to have an aromatic power disproportionate to its components: this lyrical, soaring character is shared by no other red wine, and it is the reason why wine-drinkers and wine-growers put up with so much in searching for it. Much red burgundy, even that produced during the generally affable vintages of the 1990s and 2000s and with the improved winemaking skills of today's generation, is slender and ungenerous.

Many plantings of Pinot Noir around the world are also unsuccessful. It is difficult to achieve a desirably pure, fruity amplitude in many cool climates, while warm conditions provide clumsy, sometimes jammy and sometimes bitterly extractive wines. Of the various geographical pretenders to the Burgundian crown, probably the most successful come from the well-fogged areas of California (such as Carneros and the Russian River Valley) and from New Zealand's Martinborough and Central Otago; these regularly

succeed in producing recognizably varietal Pinot with ripe yet fresh fruit backed by restrained, sweet tannins, even if the final multi-dimensional quality of great red burgundy remains elusive.

SYRAH *(Shiraz)*

Increasingly important variety grown around the world, but most particularly in France and Australia. Its home is in the northern Rhône Valley, where it produces red wines marked by deep, black-purple colors, powerful aromas (of flowers, cream, hot rubber, mulberries and black pepper) and vigorous, almost biting flavors in which bright, juicy, early-plum acidity is surprisingly prominent (the northern Rhône, after all, is not far from Beaujolais). Texturally, the wines vary from rasping (in some Cornas or Hermitage) to silky-smooth (in Côte-Rôtie). Syrah's general liveliness and go-for-it style mean that it makes balanced blends with other grape varieties such as the sweeter Grenache and earthier Mourvèdre – as it is commonly asked to do in the southern Rhône. It's charging across the Languedoc at present, chasing away Carignan and Aramon to the loud cheers of spectators.

Syrah is known in Australia (where it has been growing since 1832) as Shiraz. Quality and style depend on the site and age of vines, vinification and the commercial aspirations of the winemaker. The best Australian Shiraz is perhaps the country's finest wine of all: jet-black, oil-thick, with palate-dazzling flavors of tar, salt, dark chocolate, molasses and caramel, plus a sexy vanilla sheen from the careful use of new American oak casks. In Australia, Shiraz also blends well with the generally stiffer, more cassis-laden Cabernet Sauvignon.

Other important red grapes

BARBERA

One of Italy's great extrovert reds, grown in Piedmont, Lombardy and elsewhere. Barbera tends to be low in tannin and high in acidity, which means it tastes thin, sharp and aggressive when it's over-cropped or following a poor vintage. Yet after good vintages and when it is well-made, it is supple and pungent, quivering with vivid, high-definition plum fruit. Richly constituted Barbera takes well to oak, which fills it out and gives it a sweet sheen. It is also grown in Argentina and California, though rarely with enough care and ambition to allow clear varietal characteristics to be discerned.

CABERNET FRANC

Unlikely as it may seem, Cabernet Franc is actually one of the parents (with Sauvignon Blanc) of Cabernet Sauvignon.

Why "unlikely"? Because the red wines produced by this relatively early-budding and -ripening variety are much lighter than those of its sturdy son – yet all Cabernet Sauvignon's "red blood", so to speak, must originally have come from Cabernet Franc.

Within its French homeland, it is grown mainly in the central part of the Loire Valley and in Bordeaux, where it takes third place to Merlot and Cabernet Sauvignon. Loire Cabernet Franc (used in appellations such as Chinon, Bourgueil, Saumur-Champigny and Anjou-Villages) can be dark, but is nearly always fresh and balanced, with high levels of acidity rather than tannin structuring its brisk, raspberry fruit. In Bordeaux (and especially when blended with Merlot in the wines of Château Cheval Blanc, Cabernet Franc's apotheosis), it makes a deeper, creamier, more blackberryish wine, but still not one of great tannic substance. It responds well to oak, producing the pencil-shaving scents so typical of classic Bordeaux.

Outside France, Cabernet Franc is grown widely in northern Italy, though not every producer is prepared to make the sacrifices required to produce a red wine of even medium weight there; it can often be grassy and lean. It is extensively (though not intensively) grown by the more ambitious New World producers for "Bordeaux blend" wines, and occasionally vinified on its own to yield wines of medium depth and lively, sometimes bitter-edged or mineral-charged fruit.

CARIGNAN
(Carignano, Cariñena, Mazuelo)
A controversial red grape variety. Despite often harsh and acidic wines (generally due to over-high yields), Carignan is widely planted in France (mainly for blending in Rhône, Provence and the Languedoc) and Spain; there are extensive older plantations of it, too, in both California and South America. Many growers claim that old-vine Carignan produces worthwhile wine, and the case is most arrestingly proved in Languedoc, whose low-yielding, super-ripe Carignan can rival Italy's Amarone for invigorating, bitter-edged richness.

CINSAUT *(Cinsault)*
Good B-team variety, planted across southern France and in South Africa (where it is one of the parents of Pinotage). Its wines are lightly colored, soft, sometimes cherryish, but more often sweet-edged, even slightly toffeed. It brings scent and smooth drinkability to blends, and makes a charming rosé.

DOLCETTO
Piedmontese red variety traditionally regarded as an easy-going, sweet-edged amusement beside craggy Nebbiolo, and as a low-acidity alternative to piercing Barbera. All things are relative. In absolute terms, Dolcetto is still brisk and vivid, with lively plum and sloe characters and generous tannins. When grown, low-yielding, in the proper site and given sensitive oak treatment, Dolcetto makes a fine red wine in its own right. It is possibly related to Charbono, the beefy red grown in California.

GAMAY
An unusual grape, in that it is closely identified with one area and one alone: granite-rich Beaujolais (for the record, it is also grown with modest success in the Loire and Switzerland). Gamay produces the archetypal quaffing wine: low in tannin, high in acidity, stuffed with lip-smacking red fruit, and best drunk young. All these characteristics are amplified by the carbonic maceration technique adopted in Beaujolais; this, too, gives the wine bubblegum or banana scents, especially apparent in Beaujolais Nouveau. In the ten Beaujolais *crus* (like Moulin-à-Vent or Morgon), though, it produces a red wine of deeper (though never tannic) flavor which, with some age, can begin to resemble Pinot Noir.

GRENACHE
(Garnacha, Cannonau)
This widely planted, drinker-friendly variety is grown in southern France, Spain and Sardinia, as well as in California and Australia. As ever, how good the wine is depends, as ever, on the effort and aspiration the winemaker puts into it.

The greatest Grenache/Garnacha-based wines tend to be relatively light in color. Yet the high sugar levels this grape achieves mean that the wines are often high or very high in alcohol, and usually have an incipient raisiny sweetness of flavor and low acidity (if unadjusted) which give them a universal, easy appeal. Reduced yields and careful viticulture provide ample, soft tannins, and at best (in France's Châteauneuf-du-Pape, Spain's Priorato and warm sites with historic plantings in California and Australia) a quality of extract which gives the wines a beefy, spicy character with a long drinking window. Grenache is also used to produce strong but surprisingly drinkable rosé in France and Spain, and the sweet, fortified wines of Roussillon (Banyuls and Rivesaltes) on France's border with Spain.

can be **gamey,** or evoke the scent of crushed black olives.

LAMBRUSCO

Not so much a variety as a family of varieties grown in central Italy, where they have traditionally been used to produce dry, bitter-edged, foamy red wines, ideal for cutting the rich food eaten on the Po River plain. Internationally, however, the sweeter, simpler versions (both red and white, and generally low in alcohol) have been successful as an access route to wine for those brought up on Coca-Cola or 7-Up.

MALBEC
(Auxerrois, Côt)

Malbec is found chiefly in southwest France and Argentina. In France, it is a minor contributor to some blends in Bordeaux, adding firmness and resolution; it is more important in the dark, sometimes brusque, iron-like reds of Cahors. Argentina, too, produces good Malbec wines: these can be deep, savory and extractive, with rich yet accessible tannins framing complex, dark, earthy fruit flavors. Argentinian versions take well to oak, and age encouragingly, too, eventually coming to resemble a wilder, rumpled, slightly mineralized version of Cabernet Sauvignon. Chilean Malbec is driven by

fresher, more obvious fruit flavors and tends to have smoother tannins. The variety is also grown in Italy, Australia and California; in the last two locations it is usually blended with Cabernet and Merlot.

MONTEPULCIANO

Widely planted in south-central Italy, this amiable grape can produce deep-colored, plummy reds ideal for easy drinking.

MOURVEDRE
(Mataro, Monastrell)

Solidly textured, dense, sometimes inarticulate, high-alcohol reds are produced in both southern France and Spain by this late-ripening, heat-loving red variety. Sometimes these have a blackberry style; at other times, they can be gamey, or evoke the scent of crushed black olives. When less successfully vinified, they can be rough wines of bruising strength. The variety blends well with more perfumed Mediterranean reds like Syrah, or with sweeter-fruited Grenache and Cinsaut. There are old plantings of Mourvèdre in both Australia and California, and these produce hugely flavorful reds, well-suited to the climate of both regions: new plantings seem certain to follow.

NEBBIOLO *(Spanna)*

Challenging Italian red variety, grown in Piedmont's best sites on limy marls to make (most notably) Barbaresco and Barolo. Nebbiolo is very late-ripening, but after a long and languid late summer, it provides tannin-laden yet strangely sensual wines of depth and authority, unfolding and softening slowly in bottle. When these reach maturity, the drinker can enjoy a relatively lightly colored, powerfully aromatic red wine (tar and roses are the classic scents) with complex, persistent, autumnal flavors. Nebbiolo has traveled, but not as yet with its Italian grandeur intact.

PETITE SIRAH *(Durif)*

A Syrah/Peloursin cross, this grape produces tannic, sturdy wines in California, Mexico and Australia. These tend to be deeply colored, peppery, punchy and alcoholic, making for uniformly tannic, exciting (if abrasive) red-neck drinking.

PINOTAGE

This South African cross of Pinot Noir and Cinsaut has had a variable history, but enthusiasts feel it now produces some of the country's most exciting red wines: deep, dark, vibrantly

fleshy and richly fruited. It responds well to oak, acquiring smoky, layered complexities. Less successful versions can smell rubbery or estery.

PINOT MEUNIER

Chiefly used as one of the three authorized varieties for Champagne (and therefore vinified as a white wine). It lacks the finesse of Chardonnay and the rooty power of Pinot Noir, but adds a general sweet-apple fruitiness to blends and helps them acquire aged character relatively swiftly.

SANGIOVESE *(Nielluccio)*

Sangiovese forms the basis for all Chianti and Brunello di Montalcino, as well as for a range of ambitious Tuscan and "Supertuscan" wines, and some lighter, more easygoing reds from Romagna. Like many Italian reds, it tends to be high in both tannin and acidity; after an indifferent vintage, it will lack the central-palate richness of, say, Bordeaux-grown Merlot. Successful Sangiovese, however, makes a wine of inimitable sophistication, reminding the drinker of cherries both sweet and bitter, of plums and sometimes apples, and of coffee, leather and bay leaves. It blends happily with other varieties such as Cabernet Sauvignon and Merlot, and takes enthusiastically to new oak.

TEMPRANILLO

(Cencibel, Tinta Roriz, Tinta de Toro, Tinto Fino)

This is Spain's great red variety, used (under a variety of names) for many of the country's finest wines. It's a bit of a chameleon, capable of yielding tissue-soft charmers in some regions (Rioja or Valdepeñas) and sturdy, dense, tannic aristocrats in others (Ribera del Duero, Toro). This adaptability means that it is also a useful blending variety, and responds well to every type of oak treatment. The classic Riojan or Navarran Tempranillo-based red is dominated by fragrant strawberry flavor and vanilla-soaked American oak, whereas Ribera del Duero tends to produce darker, plum-and-chocolate fruit filled out with the more complex, pencilly aromas and flavors of French oak. It hasn't traveled with much success so far, though as Tinta Roriz it's an important contributor to port blends and some juicy Argentinian reds.

ZINFANDEL

California's "native" variety – which DNA testing has revealed to be the Primitivo grape of Italy's Puglia. In the past, it was made into relatively dark, lush, generous reds with blackberryish fruit, seldom suited to long aging. Lately, however, fastidiously non-interventionist winemakers, using very ripe, old-vine fruit, have produced wines of alcoholic wealth and sweet richness from Zinfandel; indeed, if fully ripe, this will always be a high-alcohol wine. Blends with tougher varieties (like Petite Sirah) can work well, too. Zinfandel is also made into a semi-sweet pink wine, generally labeled "blush". Thus, the taste of Zinfandel is almost entirely conditioned by the aspirations of the winemaker.

The second route to predicting and identifying what a wine will deliver is to know and understand a bit about where the wines come from. Wines reflect the places in which they are grown, so by slowly inking in for yourself a taste map of the wine world, you'll be able to anticipate a wine's flavor and style. That's the purpose of this section. We'll take a quick tour of the wine world, trying to identify the key flavors in each country or region.

Route Two:
Places

There are few greater challenges to the imagination than geology. Five million years, for example, have elapsed between the moment at which you read these words and the first hominids walked the earth. (Five million years? That's 5,000 millennia – and recently we fussed colossally over one millennium.) Yet those five million years account for very little within earth's entire geological history; it stretches back 910 times as far again into the past. For every one of that infinity of moments, geological change – extrusion, deposition, erosion – has been under way. Rivers flow; mountains crumble; lakes fill and empty; seas advance and retreat. The reality that geologists have to deal with is, even at a regional scale, impossibly complex. When you take soil as well as bedrock into account, and when you begin to examine the minute and incessant variability found within every hillside, field and pasture, complexity becomes merry anarchy.

Maps and sections are one way of trying to impose an order on the disorderly reality of geology; wine, singularly, is another. Looking at maps helps us understand geology with our eyes; drinking wine helps us taste geology – and more.

The French have a word for it: *terroir*. This means all of the ways in which a place can influence the flavor of a wine, including geology, certainly, but also including climate, aspect and topography, and even underlying local traditions of cultivation. The English neologism "placeness" comes closest to conveying the bundle of highly localized features which finds expression in the taste of a wine. Every French *appellation d'origine contrôlée* (AOC, or wine name of controlled origin) should be imbued with this placeness; it should taste of its terroir. Other European countries generally concur with the French model; the longer you grow wine in a place, after all, the more evident such subtleties become.

By contrast, in the newer wine-growing cultures of Australia, New Zealand, Chile and Argentina as well as in much of Eastern Europe, California and South Africa, there is a different philosophy of placeness. The aim there is not to produce wines whose intricacies are governed by the general or particular locale of their vineyards. In such wines, placeness is instead a framework within which a winemaker seeks to bring out memorable varietal characteristics, exquisite grape ripeness, or to express his or her own winemaking or blending skills. Nonetheless, even in those environments, placeness remains the basic reality of wine. (In general, climatic factors are regarded as more important than soil in these countries, since neighboring vineyards may be situated hundreds of miles apart.)

All wines, then, taste to a greater or lesser extent of the place in which they are grown, and the aim of this section is to help you to correlate tastes with places.

Before we start, however, a word about names. If you compile a list of the names of every region of controlled origin in France, Spain and Italy, and add to it a list containing every vineyard name you might conceivably see on the label of a bottle of German wine, you will have a document both sizable and impenetrable – and that's only four out of two dozen or so wine-producing countries. Names are a challenging aspect of wine scholarship. You will not find all those names here. What you will find are a few of the major ones, just enough to guide you on your way; for the rest, consult the specialized reference books listed in the bibliography (see page 144).

Drinking wine helps us taste geology. And more.

FRANCE

Great wine is made around the globe, between 30° and 50° latitude north and south of the equator, but France produces more great wine than any other country, for reasons both cultural and geographical. No people in the world (save the Chinese) have thrown their investigative spirit quite so wholeheartedly as the French have into food, drink and cooking. No country of equivalent size within the two wine-growing belts which circle the planet has quite the same diversity of soil and climate as France. Let's tour it from north to south.

Champagne

Northern-ness itself plays a large role in the taste of Champagne. In a cool climate, even fully ripe grapes (Chardonnay, Pinot Noir and Pinot Meunier in Champagne) will retain high levels of acidity. The still, base wines for Champagne taste – eyebrow-raisingly – like lemon juice: they are reed-slender and scalpel-sharp. Great sparkling wine such as Champagne is always made from high-acid base wines. It is that acidity, combined with the rich, cookie-like flavors left by the yeast as it completes the bubble-giving second fermentation in bottle (see page 83) and the small amounts of sugar with which the wine is "dosed" before bottling, which provides its finesse and balance. The lignite-enriched, chalky soils of Champagne have also proved ideal for producing still wines of polish and purity; the same phenomenon is evident in Cognac and Spain's sherry-producing Jerez region.

The Loire Valley

There are many tastes to the Loire Valley, yet there is a common thread to all: freshness. The freshest (providing you get them, like fish, in quicksilver youth) are the wines of the Loire's Atlantic mouth: Muscadet. The grape variety from which Muscadet is made (Melon de Bourgogne) is not hugely characterful, which is one reason why the best are bottled *sur lie*: directly off their lees. A faint breadiness then fills out their lemony pungency.

Travel further upriver and you come to that central part of the Loire known, evocatively, as *le jardin de la France* (The Garden of France). Red wines, dry white wines, sweet white wines, pink wines, sparkling wines: there's a little of everything in the varied countryside of the Anjou-Touraine garden, a region often blessed with long, languid summers and gentle, warm autumn weather.

Chenin Blanc is the chief white grape variety here, and it can pro-

duce wines of profound, orchard-like fruit with a spellbinding balance between sweetness and acidity matched only by the finest German Rieslings (which have lower alcohol). Dry versions (usually labeled "Sec") can be austere; the medium-sweet and sweet versions (labeled "Demi-Sec", "Moelleux" and "Doux") turn on the fruit-spangled enchantment. Chenin, though, can be difficult: the honey, wax, pepper, grape and dessert apple of the finest examples degenerates into raw-apple-core flavors in the less successful. Too much sulfur is another common winemaking fault.

The further upriver you travel, the more likely it is that white wines will be made, not from Chenin Blanc, but from Sauvignon Blanc, though in such cases the variety is generally specified: these tend to be crisp, bone-dry, nettle-scented and green-fruited. The sparkling *crémant* wines of the central Loire are incisive and concentrated but can be hard, lacking the finesse and subtlety of Champagne. Loire rosés are soft and often sweet. Meanwhile, the reds of Chinon, Bourgueil and Saumur are among the most brisk and fresh in France: often dark in color, they offer pungent raspberry scents and exuberant, vivid, tar-edged flavors, while acidity is generally more prominent than tannin.

The upper Loire, finally, is where Sauvignon Blanc comes into its own, on limy soils similar to those of Chablis. Sancerre and Pouilly-Fumé are names indivisibly associated with pungent, severe, almost stony whites with aromas of smoke or flowers and high-acid yet firm flavors; other appellations on the same limestone soils such as Mene-tou-Salon, Quincy and Reuilly offer similar, if slightly softer flavors. The freshness, though, remains as evident as in Muscadet.

Alsace

Alsace lies slightly further north than most of the Loire vineyards. Taste Alsace wines, however, and you might place them further south. They're still predominantly white, but there's a fullness and a roundness to most of them, their acidity often muted, which conveys an impression of plump generosity. What you're tasting, yet again, is geography. The prevailing wind across almost all of northern France is from the west, often heavy with Atlantic rain, but Alsace lies perfectly protected from these wet winds in the rain shadow of the Vosges mountains, looking down in warm sunshine on the broad Rhine Valley. Hence that roundness, that plumpness, that tenderness.

The fact that the wines are sold, California-style, by grape variety makes them an easy buy for consumers. Sylvaner, Pinot Blanc and the blend called Edelzwicker are the easy-drinkers; Riesling, Pinot Gris, Gewürztraminer and Muscat produce the majority of Alsace's greatest wines. Of these, Riesling is the most austere, full of intense, severe yet complex fruit, often requiring age to show at its best. Pinot Gris produces fat, smoky, almost oily whites with fruit-pastry flavors, while Gewürztraminer is exotically spicy and floral in scent and heady in flavor. Even supposedly dry examples of these two varieties can have a gentle sweetness to them combined with high alcohol levels, and avowedly sweet wines (labeled "Vendange Tardive", meaning late harvest, or "Sélection des Grains Nobles", meaning selected nobly rotten grapes) can be lush, unctuous and laden with sultry fruit. Muscat, strangely enough, generally produces dry wines in Alsace, with markedly grapey scents and flavors. Some Pinot Noir is also grown here to make pale, often rather slender reds.

Of all France's wine regions, Alsace has the most complex soils, and there's consequently a huge variety of minutely differentiated vineyard sites along the fractured slope which runs northwards from Thann to Wissembourg. This is one reason for the range of grape varieties; it also means that mineral flavors are apparent in a number of Alsace wines. Many of the best sites are labeled "Alsace Grand Cru".

Burgundy

In many respects, the vineyards of Burgundy are not dissimilar to those of Alsace. They also occupy east-facing, sheltered slopes looking down onto a river valley (the Saône); they, too, are geologically complex, leading to striking quality differences in wines grown in close proximity. The relief, though, is less dramatic than in Alsace, and Burgundy, of course, is further south. Serious red wine is grown here, albeit red wine of an aerial nature, while the whites are structured and vinous.

The entire region – Greater Burgundy, as it is sometimes called – is divided into four zones. In the far north lies Chablis, which geologically forms the central link in the chain of Kimmeridgian limestone joining the southerly Aube section of Champagne (planted mainly with Pinot Noir for sparkling-wine production) and the Sauvignon-growing Upper Loire vineyards of Pouilly-sur-Loire and Sancerre to Reuilly. Chardonnay is never sharper, nor greener, nor stonier than in Chablis, yet these seemingly austere, sour whites can reveal, with time, a hidden flourish of elegant richness.

The Côte d'Or is the central part of Burgundy, running south from Dijon to Santenay. This is where the greatest red and white burgundy is made, in and around a chain of often modest villages punctuated by the small towns of Nuits-St-Georges and Beaune. Nowhere else on the winemaking globe is terroir dissected and classified quite as minutely as it is here; to understand Burgundy intimately implies a lifetime's study. In broad terms, though, what are the tastes of this intricate place on earth?

Red burgundy varies from light and perfumed, full of poised strawberry fruit (from villages like Santenay or Auxey-Duresses) via a fuller yet still graceful, silky style (in Volnay or Chambolle-Musigny) towards something relatively full and sturdy, with black-cherry, mulberry or blackberry fruit (Pommard, Nuits-St-Georges, Gevrey-Chambertin). It will never have the rich substance of a St Emilion or a Châteauneuf-du-Pape, yet within its fundamentally lively style it can assume a majes-

tic breadth of flavor combined with impressive power and depth. That, of course, is when you finally find great red burgundy. Much red burgundy is thin, sharp and mean.

The best white burgundy also astonishes, though in this case the wonder is that any white wine could contain such a wide and varied range of flavors beyond the merely fruity (flowers, bread and nuts are just some of the more common allusions). Few white wines, too, ever achieve the sense of structure evident in great white burgundy, and few oaked whites are capable of such subtle expression of the vanillic, buttery, toasty potential of wooden casks. For all of this to unfold, however, white burgundies need cellar time. The basic style polarity in the Côte d'Or is between the lushness of Meursault and the flintier finesse of Puligny- and Chassagne-Montrachet. In general white burgundy tends to be more reliable than red, but there are still disappointments.

The third region of Greater Burgundy starts south of the Côte d'Or and comprises the Côte Chalonnaise and the Mâconnais. The Côte Chalonnaise is an area of fractured hill slopes whose red and white wines have a clumsiness compared to those of the Côte d'Or, though they can deliver plenty of straightforward flavor. South again, and you reach the Mâconnais, a hilly region of mixed limestone and marls predominantly producing soft, easy-going Chardonnay-based whites of no great intensity or subtlety. Yet they are still recognizably white burgundy (structured, full and more than merely fruity in flavor).

The southern end of the Mâconnais fuses with Beaujolais, the fourth part of Greater Burgundy, and here, for the first time, there is a change of fundamental soil and grape variety. Beaujolais is made from the Gamay grape, grown on granite soils. It's a pale though vivid red wine in which acidity plays a far more important role than tannin; eyes closed, a chilled glassful (and, mostly, it should be drunk chilled) could easily be white. The best Beaujolais has a juicy and thirst-quenching quality, and from some of the *crus,* or top sites (like Morgon or Moulin-à-Vent), it can achieve depth and meaty substance, though never with much tannic grip.

The Mountains

Before we leave central France, two easterly regions are worth a look: the Jura, situated on the stairway up to the Alps, and Savoie, scattered among France's higher mountain valleys. Both are small regions, and the majority of their wines are drunk locally.

The Jura's specialty is white wine given deliberate, controlled oxidation with its attendant nutty tang, and pale, light but sometimes haunting reds. In Savoie, the whites are fresher, crisper and more gracefully floral in character; the reds, by contrast, can be surprisingly dark, with iron-like, mineral characteristics.

The Rhône

The Rhône rises in the Alps, and some of Savoie's wines are grown on its banks, but this term is conventionally used to describe the wines produced in two more southerly regions. The first is that narrow part of the river valley between Vienne and Valence, the Rhône by then having been charged by the waters of the Saône. The second is the broad area centered, further south, on Orange and Avignon, shortly before the Durance swells the river to stately proportions.

The vineyards of the northern Rhône are perched on terraces and hill slopes, with a mixture of mainly granitic soil types. Whites are generally richly dry (these sites are sunny and warm), their exact character depending on the grape variety used. Those (like Condrieu) based on Viognier are profoundly floral, exotic and viscous, but most northern Rhône whites (like Hermitage and Crozes-Hermitage) are based on Marsanne and Roussanne, giving plump, apricot- or peach-suffused whites of gentle yet penetrating character. Condrieu is best drunk in its youth, while the greatest white Hermitage needs many years to reach a scented maturity.

The reds offer the purest expression of French Syrah, the soil and sites lending the variety a perfumed pungency and incisive, vivid quality it rarely achieves elsewhere. Stylistically, the wines vary from the scented, elegant intensity of Côte-Rôtie via the commanding, architec-

Chèvre fermier
Vallée d'Aspe
.133/4

Bleu au lait
de Brebis .95/4

Saint Nictaire
fermier .95/4

Sainte Victoire
fermier .85/4

Tome d'Auvergne
Croûte fleurie .85/4

Cantal doux
au lait cru
.70/4

Cantal vieux
au lait cru
.99/4

BREBIS .123/4

FROMAGES
PYRENEES de MONT

tural depths of Hermitage to the chunky, affable and savory pungency of Cornas.

Châteauneuf-du-Pape is the presidential wine of the southern Rhône, yet it is highly variable in quality, much of it being uninteresting and over-cropped, failing to justify the pompous grandeur of the AOC's heavy, embossed bottles. The fame of the name encourages easy sales. When good, however, it's the softest and most easygoing of France's fine wines: broad-shouldered, muscular and alcoholic, yet sweet-fruited and expressive, too. Its tannins, even when plentiful, are rarely hard or tough; it is ready to drink soon, but also lasts well, the very best having a "drinking window" of up to 20 years. All the reds of the southern Rhône aspire to this kind of "gentle-giant" profile, and a good Côtes du Rhône-Villages, Lirac, Gigondas or Vacqueyras can sometimes achieve it.

The region also produces generously built though mutedly characterful dry white wines (especially in Châteauneuf-du-Pape itself), strong, dry rosés and some fine, sweet fortified Muscat wines in Beaumes-de-Venise. Sadly, most remain unknown outside their localities.

the taste of wine

Bordeaux

Bordeaux is the largest producer of fine wine in France and, indeed, the world. It is renowned for its mid-weight, refined red wines, the best of which have elegant, complex flavors in which fresh red-fruit notes are perfectly complemented and balanced by cedar, spice and earth. Wines grown in this part of France often have generous, palpable tannins; acidity levels vary greatly, depending on the type of summer the region, with its maritime climate, enjoys, but after the hottest, most successful vintages, acidity tends to be low. The region is also known for subtle, dry white wines and succulent, unctuous, richly oaked, sweet white wines. Because of its huge size, however (occupying both banks of the Garonne between Marmande and Bordeaux, much of the lower Dordogne, and both sides of the enormous, swirling Gironde estuary), there are many less interesting wines, both red and white, produced within the Bordeaux area.

Red Bordeaux (known, generically, as "claret" in Britain) can be divided into two broad style groups, depending partly on the predominant grape variety used in the blend and partly on where the vines are situated. Blends on the "left bank" (the Pessac-Léognan and Graves area around Bordeaux, and the Médoc peninsula which extends northwest of the city) tend to be dominated by Cabernet Sauvignon and grown on gravel beds interlayered with sand and clay. This combination gives a brisk, almost minty style of Bordeaux, sometimes with prolific tannins, meaning that the best wines need many years' storage prior to drinking. Once mature, such wines reveal astonishing intricacies of aroma and flavor. The refined grandeur of a fully mature Médoc from a great property and a fine vintage has no peer in the wine world.

On the right bank of the Gironde, meanwhile, where Merlot is the dominant grape variety and the soils are richer, red wines tend to taste softer, with a different repertoire of fruit flavors (blackberry and cherry in place of the mulberry style of the Médoc and Graves). Right-bank Merlot tannins are often ample, but less craggy than the Cabernet Sauvignon tannins of the Médoc and Graves, so the wines reach maturity after a shorter spell in the cellar. In maturity, they retain their fruit flavors, overlaying them with a chocolatey, savory or meaty complexity.

Bordeaux's finest dry white wines are those grown in the gravels of Graves and Pessac-Léognan: these generally oaked blends of Sémillon and Sauvignon Blanc can attain the complexity of white burgundy, but their flavors are quite different, with vegetable, lemon and green-fruit notes coming creamily together. The sweet whites of Sauternes and Barsac are made from the same blend of grapes, but these gently sloping, clay-gravel vineyards situated between the Garonne and a cool tributary, the Ciron, are prone to early autumn morning mists which provoke the growth of what is called "noble rot" (*Botrytis cinerea*). This fungal disease of vines is always unwelcome in underripe fruit, but when it attacks ripe fruit it can dehydrate the grapes while concentrating their flavors, yielding rich, luscious, sugar-saturated musts. The resulting wines, after a slow fermentation, are unctuous, with a wealth of flavor interlayered with new oak and the faint bitterness of botrytis itself. They age superbly, growing in complexity over the years.

Provence, Languedoc-Roussillon and the Southwest

This vast, sunny belt of land, bordering the Mediterranean from the Alps to the Pyrenees, produces a varied scrapbook of wines. Some of these are classic terroir-influenced blends made under AOC regulations; others are vin de pays wines (such as the widely used Vin de Pays d'Oc) grown and sold as straightforward varietals. This has led to the Midi, in particular, being considered France's "New World". Such wines often lack the impact of, say, Australian or Chilean rivals, but do have a distinctively French freshness and balance.

The leading AOCs in Provence are Bandol and parts of the Coteaux d'Aix-en-Provence. Red wines here often have a savory, earthy, black-olive style: a legacy of the high percentage of Mourvèdre in the blends. Costières de Nîmes is a Rhône delta appellation where both Grenache and Mourvèdre flourish, producing red wines with a Rhône-like rich softness to them. Corbières, Minervois and the Coteaux du Languedoc are all, in part, superb vine-growing sites, and as better-quality grape varieties like Syrah, Grenache and Mourvèdre replace Carignan and Aramon, so the red wines of these AOCs improve further. The best are dark, perfumed and concentrated, seemingly flavored by the herbs which cover the remoter hillsides, and by the very stones themselves. The Roussillon AOCs are, in taste terms, a kind of cross between the sweeter wines of the southern Rhône and the more vivid, pungent, lively, thorny wines of the Languedoc hills.

Between Bordeaux and the Pyrenees, finally, lies a quilt of small vineyard areas. Those near Bordeaux (Bergerac, Buzet and Duras, plus Monbazillac for sweet whites) resemble it in flavor. The others are quite different: Madiran produces a tough red; hilly Jurançon makes piercing, fresh whites, both dry and sweet; Cahors' dark reds have a savory, mineral fleshiness to them. The simple, grassy whites made by Armagnac producers from their spare grapes (Vin de Pays des Côtes de Gascogne) can be good when young.

ITALY

In contrast to France, large tracts of which are unsuitable for wine-growing, vines thrive throughout Italy, from the Alpine north all the way to the hot little island of Pantelleria, close to the shores of Tunisia. Italy's greatest red wines rival the quality of the best Bordeaux, Burgundy and Rhône reds; its white wines, by contrast, are in general less memorable, though many make pleasant, food-friendly drinking. Since vines are grown throughout the country, and since Italy has a greater profusion of grape varieties than any other European nation, an exploration of all its viticultural nooks and crannies would require a much longer book than this. Let's take a look, though, at the most important wines of the country the Ancient Greeks called *Oenotria*, or "Vineland".

Northern Italy

Much of northern Italy is mountainous, enjoying warm but not torrid summers. Italy's freshest, most slender and perfumed white wines are those grown up in the Tyrolean heights of the Alto Adige; they have more in common with the wines of Savoie or Switzerland than the rest of Italy. In Trentino and Friuli, both lower-lying regions, white wines continue to provide most interest: here the flavors are fuller and more structured while retaining the vivid, fresh fruit which comes with a view of the mountains. In all of these areas, international varieties like Chardonnay and Sauvignon Blanc have long been planted alongside indigenous grapes, including Tocai Friuliano (Sauvignon Vert), Verduzzo and Picolit. The Schiava (Trollinger) grape produces many light, easy-drinking reds; Cabernet and Merlot can occasionally provide serious wines, though more often they are rather thin and grassy. In Lombardy, Trebbiano is used for the smooth, urbane though somewhat unchallenging white Lugana.

The most exciting wines of northern Italy are the reds of Piedmont and the valleys of Valtellina and Aosta, and the unusual reds of the Veneto. The most long-lived and intensely flavored of these are Piedmontese Barbaresco and Barolo, made from late-ripening Nebbiolo grapes grown in the sunniest marl and sand sites of the Langhe Hills. This is red wine at the limit of severity and tannic grandeur, yet it often has an enchanting floral fragrance, and a paradoxical lightness on the tongue. Nebbiolo grown up in the high Valtellina and Aosta valleys is less multi-dimensional, but can still be concentrated and intense. The more vivacious and accessible wines of the region are generally sold by grape variety: pungent, sometimes sour Barbera; softer Dolcetto and the faintly almondy white Arneis. Sweet, low-alcohol Moscato is a refreshing Piedmontese specialty which forms an absolute contrast to the region's compact reds.

The Veneto is a far more significant area in terms of volumes produced, but the quality of much of that wine is poor, including thin, sharp, under-fruited, raw reds sold as Valpolicella, and dull Soave whites. The best Valpolicella, by contrast, is cherry-scented, light and vividly engaging, packed with cherry and cherry-stone flavors. Ripasso versions are deeper, while Recioto is a strong, sweet though unfortified red produced from grapes which have been semi-dried (to concentrate sugars) before fermentation. Amarone is the dry version of Recioto and is very strong (often as high as 16 percent abv); it is still characterized by cherry/plum flavors, but here they acquire a resonant, bitter-edged intensity. Good Soave does exist, but it lacks the character of the best Valpolicella, remaining soft-fruited, nutty and full. Bardolino is an even lighter version of Valpolicella, and Prosecco is the crisp, neutral sparkling wine of the Veneto.

Central Italy

The wine styles of central Italy are diverse. There are further light, easy-drinking whites such as Rome's nutty Frascati and Umbria's slightly deeper Orvieto; over in the Marches, you'll find Italy's best fish and seafood white in crisp and lemony Verdicchio. Emilia-Romagna is perhaps Italy's greatest food-producing province and the home of its heartiest eaters; its wines are less impressive, but authentic Lambrusco (foamy, pungent, dry and rasping) is a world original, and Sangiovese di Romagna can be a juicy, jolly red. Down in the warm, hilly vineyards of Abruzzi and Molise, the Montepulciano grape is capable of making wines of rich power, with lush, plummy fruit.

Central Italy's greatest wines are Tuscan reds. Chianti is the name used to describe wines from the large area of vineyards between Florence and Siena, covering seven sub-zones; Sangiovese is the grape variety from which it is predominantly made. Anyone who knows Italian renaissance paintings will be able to visualize the typical Tuscan landscape of oak woods, stands of cypresses, olive groves, pale-stoned hilltop villages and sloping vineyards; in some ways, the refined, restrained, multi-layered flavor of Chianti itself seems to reflect that diverse landscape and the harmony which exists between its varied elements. Chianti, like Bordeaux, is generally a middleweight rather than heavyweight red. It has ample acidity and tannin, and its aromas and flavors can suggest plums, raspberries and apples, coffee, bay leaves and tobacco. The traditional Chianti "recipe" includes small amounts of Canaiolo, Malvasia and Trebbiano to lighten and thin the wine, but nowadays pure Sangiovese (and even small amounts of international varieties like Cabernet, Merlot and Syrah) are permitted.

Perhaps the most spectacular vineyard site in Tuscany is the exten-sive, warm slope stretching down beneath the town of Montalcino, just south of Siena. Brunello di Montalcino is the name of its Sangiovese-based wine, and nowhere does this grape produce deeper, denser or more sweetly fruity results. New regulations for earlier bottling than was allowed in the past have improved its quality enormously. The other major non-Chianti wine produced using Sangiovese is the variable but intermittently convincing Vino Nobile di Montepulciano.

Tuscany has also, over the last two decades, been a hotbed of great winemaking experimentation. Quality-minded producers have planted whatever grape varieties they wished (including Chardonnay, Cabernet Sauvignon, Merlot and Syrah) in whichever site they chose, usually giving the resulting wine lavish new-oak treatment, and then selling it (expensively) as *vino da tavola* – table wine; Italian wine law has not, until recently, permitted such varieties in traditional, regional blends. Such wines became known internationally, in deference to both price and quality, as "Supertuscans". The results have included some of Italy's greatest contemporary wines, and this approach has helped bring fine new terroirs, such as Bolgheri, to the world's attention.

Southern Italy

The cliché of the "two Italys" – wealthy north, impoverished south – has long been echoed in its wines, but change is coming. Few regions of Italy have improved their international reputation as substantially in the last decade as Puglia, whose Negroamaro grape and fine lime-stone terroirs are now making world-class raisiny, chocolatey Salice Salentino, Copertino and Squinzano. Campania, Basilicata and Calabria have had less export success, though the fine quality of the rich, dark-fruited, savory, gutsy reds of Taurasi and Aglianico del Vulture shows what might be achieved.

Sicily is capable of producing deep red wines and, despite blistering summer heat, fresh whites. The key is altitude: high, inland vineyards can replicate the cooler conditions in the country's northern regions. Sicily's best wines tend to be produced by ambitious individuals or companies (like the well-known Corvo); there are no great, historically sanctified terroirs. It has an extensive stock of native varieties, of which the best is probably Nero d'Avola, yielding dark, thick-textured, long-lived reds with a wild, stony, herby character (new oak gives it a sweeter, more internationally acceptable sheen). In the west of the island, Catarratto and Grillo grapes are grown to make the fortified Marsala: dry versions of this historic wine can be appealingly nutty, smooth and buttery, while sweeter ones are caramel-like and cloying.

Sardinia's achievements are less memorable, but the island produces some impressive Grenache (known there as Cannonau) and Vermentino.

SPAIN

Spain, for most wine drinkers, means two starkly contrasting flavors: the pungent, yeasty bite and oxidative tang of sherry, and the soft, gentle, vanilla-laden reds of Rioja. If you like sparkling wine, you've almost certainly enjoyed bottles of Cava, which generally comes from Catalonia. And the rest?

The rest has much to offer, though informed, adept winemaking and confidence in the intrinsic merits of Spanish wine are both recent. The world has long known France and Italy; it is only just beginning to discover Spain.

Northern Spain

This hot, dry, dusty country can indeed produce fresh whites of vivid perfume, lively fruit and restrained alcohol levels. You need to look for these in Galicia, in Iberia's far northwest. This is a little-known Spain of clouds and rain, of green pastures and forested hillsides, of deep-running river valleys and misty, vine-draped terraces. Galicia's best whites – often made with the Albariño grape variety grown on glinting granite soils – are surprisingly delicate, with peach, apricot, lemon and apple flavors. Spain's other important white-wine region is Rueda, situated further inland in Castile-León. This is a much warmer and drier area, yielding bigger, more structured white wines – yet the main grape variety, Verdejo, is good at retaining its acidity under a hot summer sun. The traditional Rueda style was for heavy, oxidized whites, but those seen on export markets today are clean, crisp, fresh and lemony. This region also produces some sinewy Sauvignon Blanc.

Perplexingly, Rueda is situated between the red-wine regions of Toro and Ribera del Duero, where some of Spain's heartiest Tempranillo-based reds are made. Ribera del Duero is Spain's boom wine zone at present: a high, limestone-soiled region whose hot days and cool nights provide reds with deep, vivid plum flavors and a firm structure which take well to oak. Some can be aggressive; all are now expensive. Toro is warmer still, yielding reds with high alcohol levels and a slightly softer style, though no less generously endowed with chewy substance.

Rioja lies northeast of Ribera del Duero, on the edge of the green Basque lands. This is Spain's Bordeaux; indeed, it was the adoption of Bordelais winemaking techniques in the second half of the 19th century that first gave Rioja an edge over other Spanish wines, and it was the disease-provoked crisis in Bordeaux, also during the second half of the 19th century, that gave Rioja its first big export opportunity.

Rioja is a large, tripartite area, comprising the Rioja Alta, Rioja Alavesa and Rioja Baja. There are clay and chalk soils, sometimes with

iron deposits, in the Rioja Alta and Alavesa, sandy soil in the Rioja Baja, and the climate throughout is one of gentle, slow and tempered warmth. The main grape variety grown is Tempranillo, with useful blending additions of Garnacha, Mazuelo (Carignan), Graciano and Cabernet Sauvignon. Stylistically, Rioja remains the home of the soft, vanilla-scented, easy-drinking red (the American white-oak barrel is the key flavor element); what modern developments have brought is greater stylistic diversity, with many more ambitious Riojas acquiring greater depth of extract and freshness of fruit. Single-vineyard wines are also common now, though the large, multi-zone blends of tradition remain the norm. Recently, white Rioja has changed from a massive, sometimes clumsily oaked, deep-golden wine to something much paler, subtler and creamier, but the grape varieties (chiefly Viura) still seem only slightly fruity.

Navarra is Rioja's neighbor, which is both a logistical blessing and a marketing curse, since its own identity has sometimes been hard to assert. Navarra's most traditional, Tempranillo-based reds are similar to many Riojas, though they sometimes show a brisker, fresher style. The region has also made a specialty of strong, though hauntingly fruity Garnacha-based *rosados*, or rosés. The last two decades have brought an increasing sense of experimentation, and this is perhaps the part of Spain where international varieties such as Cabernet Sauvignon, Merlot and Chardonnay have produced the most impressive results.

Depending on the route, a journey towards Catalonia and the Mediterranean coast will take the traveler though Campo de Borja, Calatayud, Cariñena or Somontano. Campo de Borja's wines are Navarra-like, with lots of Garnacha-based reds and rosés. Garnacha still dominates in Calatayud and (despite its name) Cariñena, but the wines tend to be much deeper, sturdier and gutsier, and are often excellent value. Beautiful Somontano is higher and wetter: Chardonnay and even Pinot Noir flourish here, producing wines of elegance (not common in Spain) and poise.

Catalonia is a microcosm of Spain: there's a little of everything there, and, of course, a great deal of one thing – Cava. Grapes for this generally inexpensive sparkling wine can actually be grown all over Spain, though most are harvested in Catalonia and almost all of the wine is vinified in a series of seven towns southwest of Barcelona. The best Cava is flowery, gentle and foamy; the worst is coarse and raw. The inclusion of Chardonnay in the blend (which is traditionally based on Parellada, Xarel-lo and Viura) is, mysteriously, controversial; it certainly seems to improve the wine to me.

Alella is another of Spain's uncommon white-wine regions; its extensive use of Xarel-lo (here called Pansà Blanca) merely serves to underline this acidulous grape's limitations. Conca de Barberà is a different story; this high, limestone-rich area produces excellent fresh, intense, red and white wines from international varieties. Costers del Segre is a semi-desert area where massive investment from the Raventós family (which runs Cava producer Codorníu) has created fine, internationally styled, richly constituted reds and

lush, lemony, oaky whites under the Raïmat label. Penedès itself is another "anything goes" area with a variety of soil, sites, grapes and wines (the more interesting wines come from the higher, inland vineyards).

Catalonia's greatest region, unquestionably, is Priorato, a fractured and chaotic landscape of hills, mountains and gorges with rocky, schistous soil, intense summer heat and, rooted between inaccessible acres of scrubby forest, some very old, gnarled and low-yielding Garnacha and Cariñena vines. Cabernet, Merlot and Syrah now supplement these to great effect, yielding red wines of enormous depth and alcoholic power, which need the influence of new oak, and which produce complex flavors of sloes, plums, blackberries, figs and licorice.

Central and southern Spain

All of the regions we've explored so far lie in the northern half of Spain. It is there, indeed, that the overwhelming majority of Spain's great wines is made. As in Italy, the south struggles. Spain's vast, arid heart, La Mancha, is Europe's largest vineyard, where modern winemaking produces some drinkable wines, but the red enclave of Valdepeñas is the only part of this zone with a tradition of quality wine. And the taste? Super-soft, well-aged, somnolent but companionable wines are traditional; newer, younger wines show more depth and brighter, plummy fruit.

Other promising areas of southern Spain include Jumilla and Yecla, where strong, gutsy, earthy reds are produced from the Monastrell grape grown in sandy limestone soil, and Utiel-Requena, where the sharper Bobal grape produces slightly lighter and brisker reds. Good (and inexpensive) fortified Moscatel wines, full of honey, orange and grape flavors, are made nearer to the sea, in Valencia.

The glory of southern Spain, however, is sherry. The grape used to make this complex fortified wine is Palomino, grown on pure, white, chalky soils in the treeless, quasi-lunar landscape around Jerez de la Frontera. It makes dull, neutral wine, but the unusual soil gives the grape some latent finesse that emerges after the special maturation processes which turn it into sherry.

There are two branches to the sherry family. One group of wines is lightly fortified to 15 percent abv and run into incompletely filled casks. A yeast mold called *flor* ("flower") soon grows over the surface of these; they will become light, dry Fino sherries, their aging conditioned by the flor. Another group of wines is fortified to 18 percent abv and aged via a process of oxidation to become dark, nutty Oloroso sherries. Amontillado is, in its purest sense, a Fino aged beyond the point at which the flor naturally dies, but the term has come to be used to describe a blended sherry somewhere in style between Fino and Oloroso. Palo Cortado is a sherry which began life as a Fino, but loses the flor to transmute, capriciously, into an Oloroso.

All pure sherry styles are dry; when they have sweetening wine added to them (generally based on molasses-like Pedro Ximénez, but pale sweet sherries are based on Moscatel), they become "creams". Consistency is assured by aging the wines in what are called *soleras*. These are large stacks of casks in which old or very old wine, in the bottom row of butts, is constantly refreshed by slightly younger wine from the butts above, which in turn is refreshed by still younger wine from the higher butts in the solera, and so on. Each year, new wine is put into the beginning of the solera, and a consistent blend of sherry of many ages is drawn off at its end.

Fino sherry tastes pungent and bracing, yeasty, and sometimes has a little gingery spice to it. Versions from Sanlúcar de Barrameda are known as Manzanilla (the Spanish word for chamomile, which these wines are thought to resemble) and taste softer and more refreshing than Jerez Fino, with an almost salty tang to them. Dry Oloroso sherry is intense, nutty and austere in flavor; Amontillado and Palo Cortado are often sweet-edged, with a faint raisiny quality interwoven with underlying nuttiness, and an occasional rice-like note, too. Very old sherries, whether dry or sweet, are the only wines to challenge vintage Madeira as the most intense wine in existence: teaspoonfuls are enough to fill the mouth with a peacock's tail of flavor. Montilla-Moriles and Condado de Huelva both produce sherry-like wines; Málaga's great specialty, meanwhile, is a dark, rich, raisin-sweet fortified wine which is now so unfashionable that extinction beckons.

The wines of Spain's Mediterranean and Atlantic islands (the Balearics and the Canaries) serve buoyant tourist demand but none are really good enough to merit export (or the inconvenience of lugging them home after a vacation).

PORTUGAL

Despite Portugal's small size in relation to its Spanish neighbor, this country nurses a passion for wine and produces a spectacular diversity of wine styles. In the north, it offers perhaps the most convincing demonstration of the importance of geography on wine flavor to be found anywhere in the world. On the map, the wine-producing area of the Minho neighbors that of the Douro. Similar wines, then? Far from it. While the Minho produces slender, tart, refreshing and low alcohol *vinhos verdes* – "green wines" – the Douro produces port, in youth the blackest, most powerful, most flavor-saturated wine it is possible to taste. The difference between the two is not just the consequence of adding brandy to port to stop its fermentation. The Minho is moist and granite-laden, a garden land where vines tangle with vegetable plots and fruit trees under cloudy and fretful skies. To get to the Douro, the traveler must cross a rock mass called the Sierra de Marão; this gathers and blocks the moist Atlantic clouds. On the other side of the mountain, dry schistous soil, prolific summer sunshine, intense heat and high, terraced slopes provide a complete contrast.

Port can be divided into two main groups, depending (as with sherry, though less radically so) on how the wine has been aged. If port is given a short spell of cask-aging before being bottled, it retains its red color and flavors of black cherry and blackberry, of pepper and fire. Simple wines of this sort are known as "ruby", while "vintage character" describes slightly darker, deeper versions of ruby port. "Late-bottled vintage" means youngish, filtered port of good quality from a single year. "Vintage port", finally, marks the summit of this particular branch of the port family: deep, rich and profound, requiring many years' bottle-aging before reaching maturity, at which point it will have thrown a heavy sediment. Most "single-quinta" ports (the word *quinta* means farm or property) are of this style, too, though often from lighter, non-classic vintages.

If, by contrast, port is aged for a lengthy period in casks before being bottled, it will be paler in color, softer and silkier in texture, and will exhibit aromas and flavors of apricot, dried fruit and nuts. Such wines are known as "tawny"; better examples include ports sold under the 10 Years Old, 20 Years Old, 30 Years Old and Over 40 Years Old categories, as well as the vintage-dated tawnies known as "colheita" ports. White port also exists, and is heady and gentle in character. Even white ports labeled "Dry" show some sweetness.

The Douro's table wines, both red and white, are richly constituted; the reds in particular can be profound, with lots of deep, dusty plum flavors. So, too, can the red wines of the surrounding Trás-os-Montes region, to the north.

The other main wines of Portugal's north are Bairrada and Dão. Despite different grape varieties and soil types (Bairrada is made from Baga grown on clay; Dão is made from several varieties excluding Baga, and is grown on sandy, granitic soil), these two red wines can be hard to distinguish. Both are deep-colored and age well, but can taste hard, acidic and astringent unless carefully vinified. Further winemaking developments should accentuate their differences in years to come.

A dozen or so wine regions jostle each other along the banks of the Tagus River inland from Lisbon (the Ribatejo), and many are still finding their identity; for some time to come, the most important information will be the producer's name on the bottle rather than its precise regional origin. Yet both red and white wines from this area can be impressive, showing the typically close-textured, naturally complex though sometimes understated flavors that seem to be the Portuguese birthright. Palmela and the Setúbal Peninsula are noteworthy for offering a range of styles, including dry Muscat wine and oak-aged reds from both Portuguese and international varieties. Setúbal is also the home of some fine aged, fortified Muscat wine.

The Alentejo is a sunny, hot region of wheat fields, cork forests and vineyards in the southeast of Portugal, near the Spanish border. Red wines from this area and its subregional zones (including Borba, Redondo, Reguengos and Vidigueira) can be soft within the Portuguese context, with deep, sweet-edged, plummy fruit.

Before leaving Portugal's table wines, its long tradition of multi-variety blends must be mentioned. The best of these (often labeled "Garrafeira") provide some of the country's most age-worthy wines.

Finally, to Portugal's second great fortified wine, Madeira. While port remains as popular as ever, Madeira has become a threatened species. The chief problem is that suitable vineland on this balmy and fecund Atlantic island, situated some 465 miles off the coast of Morocco, is under acute pressure from other crops and from housing. Wine-growing in any case had slid into decadence since Madeira's 18th-century heyday, with American hybrid varieties and the do-it-all Tinta Negra Mole grape supplanting the four noble varieties of Madeiran tradition: Sercial, Verdelho, Bual and Malmsey. Reform is in hand, but it has almost come too late.

Madeira's vines grow on volcanic soils, often in handkerchief-sized parcels on tiny terraces. The damp warmth is not particularly good for wine-growing, and the standard of viticulture on the island is often atrocious, with vines intermingled with pumpkins, potatoes and other garden crops. The base wines used for Madeira, as a consequence, taste startlingly unpromising, sour and gawky.

It is age as much as grapes, in the end, which makes Madeira. Great, classic Madeira is fortified and stored in casks kept for 20 years or more in warm lodge attics; the term "maderization" implies exposure to both air and heat. Less expensive Madeira is artificially heated for a shorter period (this process is called *estufagem*); most wines are also sweetened. At best, the island's ancient vintage wines approach an essence: piercing intensity and complexity of flavor coupled with balletic balance. That such splendid wine can be produced from such unpromising raw materials is one of the wine world's greatest enigmas.

GERMANY

Germany, I'd suggest, is the most unusual wine-growing country in the world. The fundamental balance of its wines is utterly different from that apparent, say, of wines in France or Hungary, California or New Zealand. Alcohol, tannin, structure, vinosity: forget them all. Here, a dewy delicacy reigns. No winemakers are more concerned to make fresh, fruity flavors central to the overall composition of their wines than the Germans.

As always, the place itself provides this strangely beautiful constitution. The majority of Germany's great wines are grown on perfectly exposed slopes in river valleys, sometimes dramatically narrow, sometimes broad and stately, using Riesling grapes. Riesling ripens slowly, and in these conditions it maintains high levels of acidity combined with plentiful sugars, especially when the grapes are harvested late or affected by botrytis. German winters are cold. A wine which begins fermenting in late October may not have finished the process by the time a snow-blowing north wind chills the cellar in December or January, stopping fermentation. And the result? Low alcohol levels, intense fruity acidity and unfermented residual sugar. The German wines Bach sipped by candlelight as he composed his tocatas and chorales would have tasted like that; those you or I might sip tomorrow are no different.

Several German wine regions do not conform to this pattern, though these tend to be less widely seen on export markets. Baden, for example, is the sister region of France's Alsace: the two stare at each other across the Rhine. This is by far the sunniest part of Germany, and its wines are, consequently, more alcoholic and structured than national

rivals, many of them fermented to a soft and chewy dryness. Red wines, too, are rich enough here to respond well to oak. In Württemberg, there is a tradition of easy-drinking; its wines are dryish, with a low concentration of flavor. In Franken, with its markedly Continental climate and limestone soils, wines also tend to be dry and vinous in style, yet here they have a degree of acidity which provides an arresting, electric balance and the kind of stony finesse which recalls Chablis or the Upper Loire. The wines of the small Bodensee region are similar to Switzerland's easygoing reds and whites, while those of the northerly Sachsen and Saale/Unstrut areas are like more slender, piercing examples of Franconian wine.

Germany's great classics, though, come from the slate-rich central Rhine Valley and from its tributary, the Mosel. The Rheinpfalz is the most southerly of these regions, and here, the fruit flavors are richest and ripest (peach, apricot, nectarine and orange), often with spicy notes, too. The best Rheinhessen wines (those from the red-earthed Rheinterrasse area) have a similar summer-fruit spectrum in a slightly softer, gentler style. The Nahe's ideal is one of cool, fruity limpidity and elegance, while great Rheingau wine should have remarkable intensity and definition to what is once again a broad spectrum of fresh and vivid fruit flavors. The Hessische Bergstrasse and the scenically beautiful Mittelrhein produce much smaller quantities of wine; when good, however, the best of both regions can resemble Rheingau wines. Further north, the Ahr, surprisingly, specializes in light Pinot Noir-based red wines (as does the Assmannshausen area of the Rheingau).

The Mosel Valley, finally, links the French and Luxemburg borders with the Rhine at flood-prone Koblenz; in its upper reaches, two little tributaries called the Saar and the Ruwer join it. This is where German delicacy reaches its apogee. Wines here can contain as little as seven or eight percent alcohol by volume (many beers are stronger), yet these wines can also be overwhelmingly intense and masterful, with spellbinding scents of fruit, grass and leaf, and a shocking, almost explosive grapiness. Mineral flavors, too, seem to drift like smoke through them: these are customarily attributed to the rubble of steep slate in which the vines grow. With age, the wines sometimes smell kerosene-like; the fruit spectrum deepens, yet fades very slowly.

Of course, not all German wines are made with enough care and attention to reflect these characteristics. The country also has a huge bulk-wine industry, and German wine law is so constituted that it is not easy to tell from a label whether or not a wine is produced from over-cropped vines on poor land, or from hard-pruned vines on a fine, classically steep, sunny slope. Cheap German wines are sweet, soft and insipid.

German quality-wine producers like to subdivide their crop minutely depending not only on site but on sweetness levels in the must and in the final wine, too, and this presents special label-reading challenges. *Trocken* and *Halbtrocken* mean "dry" and "half-dry"; Trocken wines, in particular, can be tart to the non-German palate. If neither of those words is visible, assume a wine will contain some residual sugar. *Kabinett*, *Spätlese*, *Auslese*, *Beerenauslese* and *Trockenbeerenauslese* are words used to describe rising sweetness levels and general richness and density of flavor. A Kabinett will be light and elegant; a Trockenbeerenauslese will be steamroller thick, unctuous and sugar-saturated. *Eiswein* ("icewine") is both very sweet and intensely acidic; it is made from frozen grapes gathered before dawn on the first profoundly chilly nights of winter. Grosses Gewächs, Erstes Gewächs and Erste Lage are terms used by some of Germany's top growers to describe wines from their greatest vineyards.

AUSTRIA
Austrian wine is produced in the low-lying, eastern regions of the country; the skiers and walkers of the mountainous west consume them. There are linguistic and some stylistic similarities between Austrian and German wines; in flavor terms, however, the wines made in the two countries are increasingly divergent. The sunshine and warmth of Austria's vineyards mean that dry wines are more successful here by international standards than from anywhere in Germany save Baden. Indeed, the quality of some oaked, dry wines produced using international varieties like Chardonnay, Cabernet Sauvignon and

Pinot Noir is good enough to cause severe detective difficulties for tasters trying to guess their origins.

The dominance of Grüner Veltliner as a variety means that Austria's most characteristic taste is of a chewy, peppery, dryish, imminently drinkable white; the best, most concentrated examples are grown on the loess soil of Kamptal-Donauland and the Wachau. Riesling from these areas can be good, too: richly constituted and intense, if lacking the ballerina-like poise of the greatest German Rieslings. The Weinviertel and the Vienna area produce straightforward whites and sparkling wines, though better things are within the grasp of the assiduous. Austria's warmest areas are those which surround the Neusiedler See, an enormous shallow lake fringed by sandy marshes which the country shares with Hungary. The mellow autumn weather common in this area means that unctuous dessert wines can be made on a routine basis (hardly the case in either Sauternes or Germany). That same warm sunshine and sandy soil have also proved ideal for producing reds of impressive depth and extract, as well as plausible, oak-fermented Chardonnay and Sauvignon Blanc.

SWITZERLAND
There are three surprises about Swiss wine. That wine-growing is possible at all in Europe's mountainous heart is the first. The second comes when skeptics taste the quality of a soft, buttery Chasselas from the shores of Lake Geneva or a ripe, dark, oak-aged Merlot from Ticino. The third and final surprise, far less welcome, is the extraordinarily high prices even Switzerland's most modest wines fetch. You need to be earning a Swiss salary to drink Swiss wine.

Wine-growing among the mountains relies

much on sunny, sheltered slopes and pockets of land, and often makes use of the power of reflected light from lake water to ripen grapes at high altitudes. The warm, dry *Föhn* ("wind") is another weapon in the wine-grower's armoury. Switzerland's appellation system, and the dozens of highly localized specialties found throughout the country resist swift summary; the general style, though, is for soft, gentle dry whites and pale, affable dry red and pink wines.

HUNGARY
Much of Hungary is suitable for vine-growing, and the country's rich stock of native grape varieties underlines the fact that this is a nation with a distinguished wine-producing history. One of Europe's greatest wines, moreover, is grown on its northeastern border, in volcanic soil and loess, and made by methods duplicated nowhere else: the sumptuous dessert wine Tokáji (or Tokay).

Furmint, Hárslevelű and Yellow Muscat grapes are, in this region of moist, warm autumn weather, regularly if partially attacked by botrytis. The rot-affected grapes may either be picked, pressed and fermented together with healthy grapes (in which case the resulting wine is known as *Szamorodni*, and is found in both dry and sweet forms), or they may be picked separately and ground to a paste called *aszú*. (The heavy drops of sugar-saturated must which seep from this paste constitute the celebrated *Eszencia*, or "essence", legendarily used to revive the dying; this syrup can barely be coaxed into a fermentation at all.) The aszú paste is mixed in with the must or wine fermented from non-botrytised grapes to provide a sweetening component and a slow, dithering refermentation. The amount of aszú used, and hence the final sweetness of the wine, is measured in

the taste of wine

puttonyos, or barrels, three-puttonyos being the least sweet and six-puttonyos being the sweetest. An Aszú Eszencia, sweeter still, is also produced. Some oxidative aging in casks was also part of the Tokáji recipe until recently, when Western European investors (including a number from Bordeaux) arrived in the region and began to make wines in which it plays little or no part. New wines from the region include soft and luscious late-harvest alternatives to classical Tokaji styles.

Tokáji has a distinctive fiery intensity to it, whether dry or sweet. Its fruit flavors embrace apple, quince and autumn fruits and leaves as well as butter, honey, marzipan and barley sugar, with oxidative versions showing a decidedly sherry-like tang. Despite the sweetness of some of the aszú wines, almost all Tokáji retains a fresh acidity which helps it age (in its distinctive half-litre bottles) superbly. Varietal table wines from both Furmint and Hárslevelű are also produced in the Tokáji region, and can be among Hungary's best: dense, chewy, and intense. Hárslevelű is more aromatic than the powerfully acidic Furmint.

Other key Hungarian wine-producing areas include Eger and the Mátra foothills, the Sopron area around the Neusiedler See (which Hungary shares with Austria), the Lake Balaton area, the Villány area in the south near the Croatian border and, finally, the Great Plain, a vast sandy expanse to the east of the Danube. Most of Hungary's wines are white, produced from a range of native and international varieties. In the former, musky scents are common, as are flavors in which soft, rich, apple-pastry fruit plays a role. They are more intriguing than Hungarian Chardonnay and Sauvignon Blanc, which make satisfactory though unexceptional wines in a light style. Hungary's latitude, often sandy soils and continental weather pattern meant that, during the pre-1989 period, its red wines rarely had any depth, substance or fat beneath their pleasant cherry and currant fruit. Ambitious younger growers, though, are now creating a range of richer, more deeply flavored reds.

ROMANIA

Like its western neighbor Hungary, Romania has a long history of wine production, a range of native varieties to call on and wine-growing regions throughout the country. Wine quality, though, reflects economic development, and in this respect Romania is moving forwards only slowly. Most of the country's substantial wine production is consumed domestically.

Soft red wines are the best buy at present from Romania: Pinot Noir, Merlot and Cabernet Sauvignon can all be soothing, modestly varietal and easy-drinking. Pinot Noir from the Dealul Mare (Big Hill) region, on the south-facing slopes of the Carpathians, represents Eastern Europe's best effort with this teasing grape variety.

Chardonnay performs well enough in Romania yielding wines with a plump, fat, well-rounded style; harder to find, but worth seeking out, are supple and succulent sweet white wines made from native varieties like Grasa and Tămîioasă (Muscat) or the native variety Tămîioasă Româneasca. Some of the best of these come from Cotnari, on the border with Moldova.

BULGARIA

Bulgaria once led contemporary winemaking in Eastern Europe but, mysteriously, the fall of communism actually reduced the quality of its wines, since much-needed land reforms languished and the vineyards were less well-maintained in the 1990s than in the 1980s. The wineries themselves are efficient, yet the quality of the fruit they have had to work with has been dismal. Bulgaria was once celebrated for its soft and curranty Cabernet Sauvignon and Merlot, as well as rounded and sometimes gutsy reds produced from the native varieties Mavrud and Melnik (Gamza tends to make a lighter red). Of the whites, Chardonnay can be acceptable, though it is sometimes over-oaked; Aligoté is often surprisingly clean and fresh, as is Muscat; while Sauvignon Blanc and Riesling are less plausible. Native whites Dimiat and Misket (both grapey and faintly musky) and the dry, sometimes intensely piercing Rkatsiteli are all worth trying if you see them.

Regional styles tend to take second place to the overall performance of key local wineries. For red wines, names to watch out for include Russe, Suhindol and Svishtov in the north, and Haskovo, Stara Zagora and Assenovgrad in the south; good whites tend to come from the east of the country (Preslav, Khan Krum, Schumen and Varna). New overseas investors, including St Emilion's Comte Stephan von Neipperg working at Ognianovo, are providing hope for the future with ripe, full-bodied reds.

GREECE

For many drinkers, the taste of Greek wine is, of course, the taste of retsina: clean and lemony wine given a haunting lilt of pine resin from the sun-filled Aleppo pine forests of Attica. Since pine has a pseudo-cooling effect on the tongue, good retsina should not be over-chilled. There is, though, much more to Greek wine than retsina.

Greece resists easy summary: its vineyards are scattered and sometimes inaccessible, reflecting the country's fractured landscape; it has a range of international and local grape varieties; and varying

levels of winemaking accomplishment. The fiercely dry heat of the Greek summer, particularly in the south of the country and on the islands, provides the opposite challenge to that faced by the wine-growers of northern Europe. Broadly speaking, its wines fall into one of two categories: traditional wines based on native Greek grapes, and small-scale, high-effort, recently founded wineries often using international varieties either alone or to complement Greek varieties.

The most rewarding of its traditional wines are the reds from Goumenissa and Naoussa in Greek Macedonia. These dark wines are based on Xynomavro grapes, and taste strong, stony and autumnal; they remind me of north Italian reds. Nemea from the Peloponnese, based on Agiorgitiko grapes, is a little softer and more cassis-like. Mavrodaphne of Patras is a dark-red, port-like, fortified sweet wine, and well-made, honey-sweet Muscat wines, both fortified and unfortified, come from the island of Samos. Other traditional wines are often regional blends put together by merchants, and are variable in quality.

Greece, though, has a flourishing "alternative" wine sector producing a range of impressive wines from both international and domestic varieties, sometimes blended and sometimes fermented as single-varietal wines. The pioneer of this approach to Greek production was Domaine Carras, situated on Sithonia, the central prong of the trident-like Halkidiki Peninsula, and producing rather raisiny Cabernet-based reds. Other noteworthy Greek reds include the dark, vivid wines of Alpha Estate in northerly Amyndeo, as well as Gaia Estate and Papantonis' Meden Agan. These last two are dark, savory, oaked wines from the Peloponnese, based on Agiorgitiko. Impressive whites include the rich Peloponnese Chardonnay made by Antonopoulos and Thessaloniki Chardonnay by Gerovassiliou, as well as the strange, mineral-flavored whites produced in the volcanic soil of the island of Santorini from Assyrtiko vines (such as Gaia Thalassitis).

ISRAEL

Kosher strictures of varying severity impose handicaps on Israeli wine-makers, and the traditional, sweet styles required for family religious use are distant from contemporary taste. Yet Israel can produce commendable dry varietal wines, particularly from the occupied territory of the Golan Heights, where temperatures are cool enough to keep genuine freshness in the grapes. Cabernet Sauvignon and Merlot from this annexed region of Syria have a smooth, chocolatey depth and impressive natural balance and poise, and Chardonnay is not far behind. Red wines from the hotter plains of Samson and Samaria (Shomron and Shimshon) tend to show dried-fruit rather than fresh-fruit characters, though they have depth, while dry whites are, with careful vinification, clean and full-flavored (dry Muscat can be particularly good). The Carmel cooperative dominates production.

LEBANON

Lebanon's wine-growing is centered in the Bekaa Valley, to the east of Mount Lebanon and, like the Golan Heights further south, the Bekaa's height helps moderate what would otherwise be extremely hot growing conditions. Lebanon's outstanding producers include Château Musar, whose red blend of Cabernet Sauvignon, Carignan and Cinsaut is one of the wine world's great originals, as well as the long-established Kefraya and Ksara, and ambitious newcomer Massaya.

OTHER EUROPEAN, EURASIAN AND NORTH AFRICAN COUNTRIES

Wine-growing in England and Wales has been only a partial success owing to the unpredictability of the summer weather there. The best wines, though, (many of them based on hybrid vines such as Seyval Blanc or German crossings such as Huxelrebe, Müller-Thurgau or Reichensteiner), have elegant meadow scents and intense, silvery flavors of grapefruit, apple and lemon. Sparkling wines based on Chardonnay, Pinot Noir and Pinot Meunier produced on the chalk-and-greensand soil of Kent, Surrey and Sussex are promisingly incisive.

Slovenia produces fresh whites and light, juicy reds, as well as much dough-soft Laski Rizling; Croatia's best wines are probably the soft, earthy reds of the Dalmatian coast based on the Plavac Mali grape variety. Montenegro's top wines are red, too, from Vranac this time. The Zilavka grape of Bosnia-Herzegovina can produce haunting, scented whites in the Mostar area, while Macedonia has good potential for both red and white wines based on Vranac and Traminer grapes. Serbia has not produced much memorable wine; recently it specialized in producing cheap, sweet red for the German market.

Both the Czech Republic (in Moravia) and Slovakia can produce convincing, almost Alsace-like whites; Slovakia has a morsel of the Tokáji region, too. Moldova produces a vast amount of wine, but quality is still patchy; the Crimea in the Ukraine enjoys a distinguished history of dessert-wine production dating back to Tsarist times; and Russia's Black Sea vineyards have potential, but only that as yet. Georgia has a wealth of native grape varieties, but its antique winemaking methods render many of them inscrutable and inarticulate. Recent Western help, however, has produced some deep-flavored, vividly fruited reds based on the Saperavi and Mtsvani grape varieties grown in Kakheti, to the east of the country.

To date, Cyprus has been unable to recover from its history of mediocre vineyard management and imitative winemaking; its only outstanding wine is the unfashionable brown, sweet Commandaria. Turkey has vast vineyard areas for dried-fruit production, but its wines are undistinguished. Morocco produces some of North Africa's best wines, both red and rosé, including delicious Carignan (made by carbonic maceration); Tunisia, too, can make earthy, intense red wines and the more traditional sweet Muscat wines. Algeria has the remnants of a once-thriving French colonial wine industry, but plantings are diminishing rapidly, as indeed they are throughout North Africa.

There are small pockets of land in India, Japan and China where vines are grown and palatable wines made, generally based on international varieties and styles (and including, in Japan, a number of wines based on blends of locally produced wine with imported wine and must). The only impressive wines from these three countries so far come from Japan (including botrytis-affected dessert wines), and have been created with extraordinarily painstaking viticultural and winemaking stratagems in this difficult, rainy climate.

NORTH AMERICA

The first Europeans to explore the northern reaches of North America were almost certainly tenth-century Scandinavians. Two of their sagas relate the discovery of the land they christened *Vinland*, so named because of the profusion of wild vines found there. Other, later colonists from France, reaching the continent at its most southerly point, described similar scenes; and it was the descendants of those vines which later saved the wine world when the root-eating phylloxera pest threatened to destroy Europe's wine vine, *Vitis vinifera*, in the late-19th century. Almost every vine in Europe today is grafted onto a phylloxera-resistant rootstock derived from American vine species.

Given this ancient acclimatization of the vine in North America, it's no surprise that small-scale winemaking takes place in almost every state of the US, and in Ontario and British Columbia in Canada, too. Only California, Washington, Oregon and New York State, however, are important in terms of quantity.

New York State

The wines of New York State are in transition; in the past, most were made from hardy American vine varieties or hybrids and thus had limited export potential. Wines from American vines have a fruit-juice-like simplicity of flavor, often with musky or foxy tones, while hybrid-vine wines may be more inoffensively palatable, but they still lack the compelling quality of even ordinary vinifera wines. All of New York's best wines are now made from these vinifera varieties; they include impressively cassis-laden Merlot and Cabernet Franc from Long Island, and Chardonnay and Riesling from sites in the traditional upstate vineyards.

California

Of the remaining three states, California is dominant, producing 90 percent of the country's wine. Much of this is grown and processed on an industrial scale by the world's largest producer, Gallo, using Central Valley fruit to make easygoing, semi-sweet white and pink (though the perception that red wine is better for health than white has led to a surge in its popularity). California's quality wines, by contrast, are produced in a much greater variety of vineyard sites by a profusion of small-scale (and sometimes microscopic) enterprises.

Europeans tend to assume that, in California, north is cool and south is hot, whereas this principle has only limited application here. A better rule of thumb is that coastal is cool and inland is hot. A cold ocean meets a warm landmass here, and the result is fog, which keeps the coastal areas chilly — and some inland areas, too. Fog aside, the climate is warm and vine-friendly, with long growing seasons.

A system of American Viticultural Areas (AVAs) has got the search for terroir under way, though in truth most Californian wines still reflect the aspirations and predilections of the owner and winemaker more clearly than the soils and slopes in which the vines grow. Winemaking styles are in constant evolution, and the trend among smaller, quality-conscious producers is increasingly non-interventionist, allowing the growing season and the grapes to express themselves without fussy technical corrections. This nearly always results in wines of great breadth and stature, often with a terrific alcoholic charge, full of soft, sweet-edged flavors and ample, supple tannins. ("Fresh" varietals like Sauvignon Blanc or Cabernet Franc are in general less successful than the intrinsically richer varietals such as Chardonnay, Viognier, Cabernet Sauvignon and Zinfandel.) The scale and generosity of California is reflected in its truest wines. Larger producers, by contrast, tend to

"design" their wines according to the perceived requirements of the consumer, giving them a more international, though simpler, style.

California's most celebrated wine region, the Napa Valley, lies northeast of San Francisco and, despite being relatively short (20 miles from one end to the other), it grows steadily warmer as inland Calistoga nears and its cool, foggy ocean access is left behind. Napa's hallmark is effortless breadth in all its wines, particularly majestic, big-boned Cabernet Sauvignon and sumptuous, silky Chardonnay. Napa Merlot, on the other hand, can sometimes be a bit too chunky for its own good. Sonoma Valley, adjacent to Napa, has more heterogeneity of style, and its best wines have greater delicacy. South of both lies Carneros, a cool and windy region where some of North America's best Pinot Noir and most naturally restrained Chardonnay are grown. Knights Valley, Alexander Valley, Dry Creek Valley and Russian River Valley lie

route two: places

northwest of the Napa and Sonoma Valleys, and offer further nuances and variations. Especially good are the rich Dry Creek and Alexander Valley Zinfandels, which seem to have greater complexity and depth of flavor than most (Ridge's celebrated Lytton Springs and Geyserville are sourced here), while Chardonnay and Pinot Noir flourish in the cool and foggy Russian River Valley (and its Green Valley offshoot). North again, and Mendocino offers a bit more of everything, with some promisingly chilly sparkling-wine country near its coast in the Anderson Valley and warmer conditions for Chardonnay and Zinfandel further inland. North Yuba, on the way to Nevada, is hot.

South of San Francisco lies another chain of inland vineyard sites showing the same stark climatic variations depending on how direct their access to the sea is or how high up a mountainside they are. One of California's most celebrated Cabernet vineyards, Ridge's Montebello, is located at a relatively cool 1,969 feet in the Santa Cruz mountains south of San Francisco Bay. York Mountain and Paso Robles are warm, dry-grass Zinfandel and Cabernet country, whereas Edna Valley and Arroyo Grande can make fresh Chardonnay and sparkling-wine base wines. Parts of the Central Valley (Lodi and Madera) offer sweet, unctuous Zinfandel, and good dessert-wine or fortified-wine grapes, if yields are kept low.

Oregon and Washington

Climatically speaking, Oregon is a more difficult place to grow grapes than California. It's cool and wet, with unpredictable summer and autumn weather. No surprise, then, that the world's most fickle grape variety, Pinot Noir, should have felt at home there. The results, as in Burgundy, are variable, but the best Oregon Pinot Noirs are true to type: close-textured and complex. Oregon's finest Chardonnays are creamy, deft and brisk; the worst are lean. Pinot Gris is a newer arrival, producing soft, pear-fruited wines.

Washington is an astonishing region to visit for those more familiar with Europe's painterly vineyard landscapes. Vines here form islands of green in a vast, bare and terrifying desert-like landscape cut by deep and thundering rivers, and exposed to a merciless, continental climate of freezing winter chills and burning summer heat. The region produces satisfactory Chardonnay and Cabernet Sauvignon in which relatively high alcohol levels are matched by fresh acidity and fruit flavors; the surprise, though, is how well Merlot performs in this most un-Bordeaux-like of environments, producing dark, sumptuous, chocolatey wines of sometimes thrilling depth and definition.

Canada

Canada's wine production, concentrated in Ontario but with a presence, too, in British Columbia's Okanagan Valley, challenges preconceptions. Pinot Noir, Merlot, Riesling and Chardonnay can all produce wines of modest depth, true ripeness and enjoyable precision of flavor; yet, unsurprisingly, it is Icewine of little subtlety but arresting intensity, from both Riesling and the hybrid variety Vidal, that has caught the world's attention.

CENTRAL AND SOUTH AMERICA

Mexico, the oldest wine producer in the Americas, has sizable vineyard acreages, though the majority of its vines produce fruit for eating, drying and brandy production. Its wines are, however, better than a cursory glance at the map might suggest: Cabernet Sauvignon and Petite Sirah, for example, both achieve effortless ripeness and display warm, sweet-edged fruit characters here. **Brazil's** wine industry is large, but so far, results are less internationally competitive from this semi-tropical climate; the wines of **Peru** are a curiosity. **Uruguay** is more promising, both for international varietals like Chardonnay and Cabernet, and for interesting wines from the local specialty, Tannat.

And then there's **Chile**. It is only in the central, Mediterranean-climate zone that vines flourish – and flourish is the right word. A clockwork climate; lush, loamy soil; ample irrigation water... the formula is perfect for high-volume, industrial viticulture. Yet even the most inexpensive Chilean wines tend to taste more impressive than that description might suggest. Red wines in particular, from Cabernet Sauvignon, Merlot and Carmenère, have a glorious fruit character, a roundness, a ripeness, a natural balance and an easy sympathy with oak which sets them apart from any other southern-hemisphere competitor. This soft and singing quality is lent freshness and complexity by new hillside and coastal sites in areas such as Colchagua (Apalta) and San Antonio. The most common fault in Chilean reds is a green, herbaceous quality.

Chile has had less success with white wines, but Chardonnay has improved over the last few years and a soft and creamy style (much of the flavor coming from winery work on oak and lees) is now the Chilean norm. New coastal plantings in Casablanca, Leyda and San Antonio are giving white wines (based on Sauvignon Blanc, Gewürztraminer and Viognier) with marked freshness and ripely citric appeal. Red varieties (including Syrah) from these areas are fresh and lively, too.

The backdrop to every Chilean vineyard is a magnificent prospect (sadly often rendered hazy by smog and traffic fumes) of

the snowy Andean peaks. Cross them, and you'll find a wine industry which should, in many ways, be a mirror image of Chile's. There's the same regular growing season, the same ample water for irrigation. Yet the wines of **Argentina** taste very different to those of Chile.

There are, in fact, key differences. The soil in Argentina is sandier and thinner, and there are greater climatic variations between the growing regions. In general, the climate is continental in Argentina, compared with the gentler, Mediterranean-style warmth of Chile. Most main Argentine wine-growing regions, especially those sited at 3,280 feet or more, balance hot summer days with cool night-time conditions. Argentina also has a more distinctive grape profile than does Chile. Its dry, spice-scented white grape Torrontés, for example, is widely grown in the northerly Salta region, though in time it will be balanced by those red varieties which perform well there, too, especially the rare Tannat. Malbec, Argentina's great red grape, finds what is perhaps its favorite world location outside France in Mendoza. Here it produces thick-textured, extract-laden, peppery, earthy wines which make the perfect accompaniment to the superb beef of the pampas. Argentinian Malbec, too, blends well with other varieties, lending them depth and texture. Cabernet Sauvignon, Merlot, Syrah, Tempranillo and Bonarda also do well here: the first three generally follow the gutsy Malbec path, while the final two tend to be vinified in a juicier style. Argentinian Chardonnay and Sauvignon Blanc are still finding their feet, though Mendoza Chardonnay shows peachy promise; the cool Patagonian region of Río Negro may prove propitious for these white varieties, though it also looks good for fresh, fruity, soft-textured Merlot and Malbec.

SOUTH AFRICA

The vineyards of Cape Province have traditionally been found within large estates of remarkable scenic grandeur and evident historical wealth. These estates, bathed in clear, bright light, are the chief nodes in a village-less rural landscape. Change, though, is coming: the creation of new, smaller wineries and the development of previously unexploited vineyard areas has made the Cape excitingly unpredictable over the last decade.

The taste of South Africa, too, is harder to pin down than that of rival southern-hemisphere countries, though the wines often have a natural freshness, and an aptitude for aging, which eludes some of their competitors. Most familiar to modern export consumers are the country's inexpensive and easygoing white wines, a reminder of the large brandy industry the nation once ran. White grape varieties, especially Chenin Blanc and Colombard, still outnumber red, and with careful vinification these can be made to an internationally popular, gently off-dry style.

The majority of the country's red wines, and the more serious white wines, show marked and promising regional variations. The coolest wine-growing regions hug the southern coastline: historic Constantia adjacent to Cape Town itself, and Elgin, Walker Bay and Elim further east, are capable of producing crisp and crunchy Sauvignon Blanc full of ripe, appley fruit, poised and elegant Chardonnay, and complex, delicate Pinot Noir. Stellenbosch is a large zone with some coolish, coastal estates but also warmer zones further inland; hence there's a bit of everything here, but reds are particularly noteworthy.

Paarl is generally hotter than most of Stellenbosch, and fortified wines have a long tradition here. Its top estates, though, produce ambitious varietals to rival the best of Stellenbosch, including some impressive, if heavyweight, Chardonnays. Worcester and Robertson, further inland in the Breede River Valley, are hotter still; Robertson's limestone soil, however, can produce some excellent, creamy and surprisingly subtle Chardonnays. Newer areas of promise include Swartland, ideal for gentle, full-flavored reds; high altitude Cederberg for wines of complexity and intensity; the fresh, cool Darling Hills and the super-cool Cape Point.

South Africa's years of isolation left it a legacy of varietal and clonal stagnation and ill-conceived winemaking ideals. Virus-affected vineyards remain problematic, but a flourishing spirit of creativity in South Africa has produced competitive wines at every price level. South Africa's greatest reds are now deep, poised and long-lived, marked by genuine elegance in place of the clumsiness of the past; while its greatest whites show not only remarkable varietal fidelity but well-judged, restrained winemaking craft.

AUSTRALIA

No other country in the southern hemisphere has made an impact to rival that of Australia on the world winemaking scene over the last two decades. This is not due to the potential of its best sites, considerable though these are, but rather to the technically proficient, ruthlessly pragmatic and highly professional Australian approach to winemaking. The best Australian wines have an unmistakably clean, bright stamp to them, and a core of ripe, vividly defined fruit. This is the result of that pragmatic and assertive winemaking, combined with the generous sunshine most Australian winemaking regions enjoy. There is also a long tradition of producing inter-regional blends in Australia for consistency and regularity of flavor.

Most Australian wines are sold as varietals, and where strong regional traditions have developed, these are generally associated with one or two specific grapes. Climate is regarded as being more significant than soil in most regions of Australia.

New South Wales and the Capital Territory

The majority of Australia's pioneering 19th-century viticulture took place in New South Wales and it still has, in the Hunter Valley, one of the most distinctive Australian wine-growing environments. Within the Australian context, it's tricky, with unusually copious summer rain. Semillon is the grape variety most closely associated with the Hunter and it provides (often unoaked) white wines which are rather inarticulate in youth but which, with age, acquire complex aromas of lemon, toast, honey and even lima beans and cheese. Their flavors never seem quite as complex as their aromas, but are vivid and characterful nonetheless. Chardonnay, though, is more widely planted than Semillon here, and produces a rich, pollen-scented, honeyed style; Cabernet Sauvignon and Shiraz can both be soft, lush and savory, again with good aging potential. Other major areas in New South Wales include Mudgee (firm, focused reds and whites), Cowra (peachy Chardonnays), Riverina (a bulk-producing area noted for botrytis-affected Semillon of great intensity but little subtlety) and the cooler district of Orange (elegant, fresh whites). The Capital Territory of Canberra, too, produces fine cool-climate reds and whites of perfumed polish.

Victoria and Tasmania

Wine production is scattered throughout the southerly state of Victoria; many "regions" are, in effect, composed of just one or two wineries producing a full spectrum of reds and whites. This makes it the most difficult of Australia's states to generalize about.

The fortified Muscats, Tokays (Muscadelles) and "port" styles of hot Rutherglen and Glenrowan are the state's ancestral wines. The unctuousness, gentle tang and massive sweetness of these cask-aged blends make them memorably unique. Up, too, in the warm, neighboring zones of Murray-Darling and Swan Hill (shared with New South Wales), enormous vineyard areas draw on irrigation water from the Murray River to produce relatively inexpensive wines cast in the brightly flavored Aussie mold, though better quality wines are possible there if growers are prepared to limit yields.

Sparkling wines have long been a Victorian specialty, using cool-climate fruit from higher vineyards in the west and south of the state. Shiraz and Cabernet Sauvignon from western Victoria have a good reputation for perfume, spice and brisk elegance; in the slightly warmer conditions of central Victoria (Heathcote and Bendigo), these varieties give a richer, deeper, more earthy style. The Goulburn Valley is renowned for powerfully flavored, cream-and-apricot Marsanne.

Head for the coast, meanwhile, and you'll find some of mainland Australia's coolest growing environments. Sparkling wines achieve real finesse in the Yarra Valley east of Melbourne; Chardonnay and Pinot Noir are also widely grown here and in the nearby Mornington Peninsula to yield wines of delicacy, poise and concentration. Fresh, peppery Shiraz is made both in the Yarra and just north of Melbourne, in the Macedon Hills. Cross to Tasmania, and conditions grow cooler (and windier) still; incisive sparkling wines seem to be the island state's natural vocation, but increasingly ripe and balanced Chardonnay and Pinot Noir are also produced.

South Australia

This is the country's leading wine state in terms of both volume and quality. Coonawarra, in its cool far south, is front-runner for the accolade of Australia's leading Cabernet Sauvignon and Merlot zone: red soil over a limestone calcrete base, plus long, lingering maritime summers provide penetratingly mulberryish, intense wines with peppery, tannic depths. In warm vintages, Coonawarra Shiraz is no less pure and intense, while Chardonnay and Riesling can be tangy, earthy and deep. Nearby Robe and Koppamurra are new additions to what is now known as the "Limestone Coast"; the longer-established region of Padthaway, celebrated for its structured, chewy Chardonnays, is also included in this designation.

Adelaide itself is surrounded by wine-growing regions. McLaren Vale and Langhorne Creek lie south of the city, basking in sunshine, their vineyards often fringed by wild olives. Both of these areas produce the kind of gut-bucket, depth-charging Shiraz reds which have made Australia's name. Cabernets from here are fine, too, with a more focused, tightly meshed fruit style; and Grenache acquires a syrupy

depth and spicy, sweet-plum power it can rarely manage anywhere else in the world. Whites, by contrast, can be over-weighty.

The Adelaide Hills provide some of Australia's most beautiful vineyards; their height, 1,300-1,968 feet above the city, means they are cooler and damper than Adelaide itself. White and sparkling wines from this recently developed area show restrained, pure-fruit characters. The Adelaide Plains, by contrast, are hot, and yield richly textured reds.

The long-planted Barossa Valley is home to what are, for many drinkers, Australia's archetypal wines: black, powerful, fleshy, salty, ashy reds, which almost seem to have been mined from the earth rather than pressed from fruit. Shiraz is the great Barossa variety, happily at home for well over a hundred years and deeply content in the burnt, mineral depths of the dry valley floor, but Cabernet, Grenache and Mourvèdre (Mataro) can also be good, as can fortified wines. The neighboring Eden Valley is slightly cooler, producing a fresher style of red wine, classic Chardonnay and intense, citrus-fruit-flavored Riesling.

Riesling is still more important in the Clare Valley: its pithy, zesty examples age superbly. Clare Chardonnay has an almost Riesling-like intensity and vividness, yet finely balanced, multi-dimensional reds are typical, too, of this expanding, impressive region. The Riverland area of the Murray Valley, by contrast, is the source of huge amounts of straightforward, high-yielding fruit for Australia's big-blend brands.

Western Australia

The wineries of Western Australia, finally, justify their high prices with complex, close-textured flavors and an intense clarity and definition that seem, so far, to reflect the pure maritime air in which the leaves unfold, more than the soil which the roots grasp. Some of Australia's most polished, intricate, multi-layered, finely balanced and age-worthy Chardonnay and Cabernet come from Margaret River; limey Semillon and cindery Shiraz can be good, too. Western Australia's other areas are widely scattered, from the Swan Valley near Perth to the Great Southern region near Albany. In general they produce wines of slightly less intensity but a similarly fresh, well-balanced style with focused, vivid, sometimes explosively bright fruit.

NEW ZEALAND

New Zealand lies well to the south of the main centers of southern-hemisphere viticulture in Chile, Argentina, South Africa and Australia; only Tasmania has a geographical situation in any way similar. It's small surprise, therefore, that the wines of New Zealand taste markedly different from those of its southern peers.

The country is overwhelmingly a white-wine producer, and the general flavor of New Zealand is vivid, clean and fresh with zippy, sherbety fruit (often lemon and lime) of striking intensity. No one who has visited the country can forget the dazzling clarity of the air there and the brightness of its light. The fact that rainfall is plentiful (promoting leaf growth) finds its counterpart in the attractively and ripely herbaceous flavors evident in some wines. Canopy management – achieving the optimum ratio and positioning of leaves to fruit – has been New Zealand's great gift to world viticulture.

The country has three dominant areas: Gisborne (Poverty Bay), Hawke's Bay and Marlborough. Many of New Zealand's least expensive whites begin life in Gisborne; its best wines are soft and peachy Chardonnay and mild-mannered Gewürztraminer (it has some of the spice of French models, and increasingly shows their vinous fire, too). Hawke's Bay has a variety of different subregional conditions, and this is where many of the country's top Chardonnays are made. These have great depth and intensity of tight fruit, and respond well to oak, which lends them a creamy succulence. Hawke's Bay Sauvignon Blanc is generally mellower, softer and suppler than that of Marlborough, with nectarine or green-plum flavors. Cabernet Sauvignon, Merlot and Cabernet Franc can perform well here in most vintages, producing dark, fresh, pungently curranty, lean reds but less successful examples show a herbaceous greenness. The country's most impressive Cabernet Sauvignon, though, is grown on warm, dry Waiheke Island, near Auckland itself. These wines have a ripe breadth to them, combined with the usual New Zealand clarity of bright fruit flavor.

Marlborough is now New Zealand's biggest vineyard area, despite the fact that the first vines only went into the ground there in 1973. The driving force behind its success has undoubtedly been its pungently grassy, gooseberryish Sauvignon Blanc, though increasingly impressive Pinot Noir looks like adding a new string to its bow. The bolt of vivid, zingy acidity which runs through most Marlborough Sauvignons has near-electrical force, and again seems to reflect the bright sunlight and clear air in which they grow (though Marlborough also benefits from some stony, dry riverbeds as vineyard sites). Subtle oaking and lees contact adds a pleasing layer of cream to a minority of these wines. Marlborough Chardonnay is often limey, and, of course, oak fills it out more frequently than Sauvignon; Riesling can provide a greater spectrum of fruit flavors, both in dry and sweet (botrytis-affected) versions.

New Zealand's most successful red wines seem certain to be its Pinot Noirs, many of them coming from the Martinborough region (Wairarapa) at the southern end of North Island. Pinot, here, can produce a wine of perfume, balance and depth. Canterbury, too, can produce fine Pinot as well as elegant, brisk Chardonnay, and Nelson is known for both Chardonnay and Riesling. Central Otago, finally, is where you'll find the most southerly vineyards in the world; in contrast to every other part of New Zealand, its climate is not maritime but continental, with hot summers and cold winters. Pinot Noir is again the grape of choice, and the fruited purity and poise of the best of these are already challenging the best of Martinborough.

The third main element in the creation of wine flavor is the role of human beings themselves. Nature is the source of aroma and flavor, but winemaking prowess is crucial in ensuring that drinkers get to appreciate the best of what nature has to offer. Poor vintages, too, need great winemakers to redeem them. Our third route, then, to understanding how wines will taste, is to trace the ways in which people can influence flavor, beginning in the vineyard and following the process through to bottling and aging. This will, in particular, help you to decipher back labels, which frequently describe the techniques used to produce the wine.

Route Three:
People

So far, our quest for wine flavor has led us to look at grape varieties and the places in which grapes are grown. Both have a major impact on flavor. Grape varieties are, if you like, the genes of a wine; the place on earth in which a vine grows provides its family context, its upbringing and its environment. Yet no untended vine ever fruits successfully, no grapes ever crush themselves, and no vatful of juice ever oversees its own fermentation before slithering unaided into wooden barrels and glass bottles a few months later. It is human beings who perfect or squander the potential of grapes and the places in which they grow. They are, to continue our analogy, the educative force working on a wine. An understanding of the ways in which humans affect wine is our third route to discovering how and why wines taste the way they do.

Grape varieties are, if you like, **the genes** of a wine.

THE VITICULTURIST

Over the last two decades, winemaking has been regarded as the main influence on flavor. Today, however, there's an increasing realization that the man or woman growing the grapes – the viticulturist – is just as important as the winemaker, and quite possibly more so. Only great grapes, after all, make great wines.

The principles of good viticulture are relatively straightforward; the bitterest part of the work is responding to what can be catastrophic problems and difficulties. These will be examined later, but first, let's look at vineyard conditions in an ideal world.

Generally speaking, vines like warm, sunny climates of the Mediterranean type, with sparse summer rain; and they like to grow in relatively poor, stony, well-drained soils. Beyond that, the variables are so

numerous that it is hard to generalize with any usefulness. In cool climates like those of Germany or northern France, the best sites are on perfectly exposed, south-facing hillsides. These maximize exposure to sunshine and allow excess moisture to drain away (and cold air to slide away on frosty nights). In much hotter climates, the best sites might be elevated or facing away from the sun so as to temper excessive heat; and for vineyards which need irrigation (like most in Australia and Chile), soil with some water-retaining capacity may be a benefit. What matters is an intimate understanding of the site so that fruit of the desired quality can be produced.

There are many different ways of training vines, and once again, the requirements of both sites and varieties vary considerably. One basic principle is that an increase in cropping levels will lead to a dilution of flavor. Another is that in most climates, leaf-shaded fruit will have unwanted herbaceous flavors and may only achieve partial ripening. Winter pruning and "green harvesting" (cutting off unripened bunches of grapes in midsummer) are important in reducing yields; "canopy management" (trimming the leaves and shoots of the vine to allow optimum levels of light and air to reach the grapes) helps bring out the ripe fruit flavors most drinkers like. Old vines (an unregulated term usually signifying vines of between 30 and 100 or more years) are thought to produce wine of high quality, partly because they are naturally shy yielders, and partly because their roots penetrate deep into the subsoil, and this, too, is considered to add complexity of flavor. Such wines are labeled "Vieilles Vignes" – "old vines" – in France.

Harvesting, obviously, is a crucial time. Assuming steady, fine, early autumn weather, the ideal moment to pick is when the grapes acquire full ripeness. Underripe grapes are

occasionally picked either by necessity (due to weather problems) or choice (in hot regions where sparkling wines, or wines with a characteristically fresh, keen-edged profile, like Sauvignon Blanc, are required). Underripe grapes, though, seldom make good wine.

Grapes are sometimes deliberately left to overripen, too. In the Merlot-growing regions of Bordeaux, for example, this technique has sometimes been adopted to make richly textured, lush, low-acid reds. More commonly, it is used to create classic dessert wines. Late harvesting sometimes implies the action of botrytis, or noble rot (see page 124), but also involves the simple shriveling of the grapes by fierce sunlight. Viticulturists also occasionally allow grapes to dry and shrivel after harvesting but before fermentation – for example, to make Recioto and Amarone in Valpolicella.

What of the problems and difficulties I mentioned above? First of all, ripe grapes taste delicious to a variety of creatures from parrots (in Western Australia) to baboons (in South Africa) and wild boars (in Champagne and Germany); physical barriers such as fencing or netting are the only means of keeping the wild and hungry at bay. Pests and diseases also besiege grapes, just as they do every worthwhile crop. The two greatest challenges viticulture has ever faced were oidium,

or powdery mildew (which decimated France's vineyards in the 1850s, and was overcome by using sulfur dusts or sprays), and phylloxera (see page 60). Other common diseases are downy mildew, botrytis itself (unwelcome on all grapes except those destined for dessert wine) and viruses; chemical sprays are the almost universally-used preventative measure; even within organic viticulture, sulfur preparations are permitted. Grape pests include moths and mites, also controlled with chemicals (including pheromones).

Attacks by the weather, however, can be even more catastrophic than a flock of parrots or a dose of powdery mildew. A severe winter chill (of −30°F or more) will kill vines, but this is rare in most wine-growing regions. Spring frosts are more frequently the villains, killing off delicate bud growth, and thus drastically reducing or even obliterating the harvest, while hail can physically damage fruit, provoking rot. Rain, especially at harvest-time, is a perpetual problem in many of Europe's vineyards; the quality of potentially great vintages has often been diluted into mediocrity by a week of downpours. Sometimes the summer is just not warm enough to ripen grapes fully, but it can also be too hot, and in fiery drought conditions vines shut down their reproductive cycle and concentrate on survival alone,

meaning once again that the fruit refuses to ripen fully.

What can viticulturists do to minimize the damage from such climatic hazards? They can protect their vines against spring frosts by using small stoves to warm the air, windmill fans to circulate air, or spraying the buds with water (this forms a protective coating of ice over the bud). Hail clouds can occasionally be seeded with rockets to provoke them into discharging their cargo of icy pellets elsewhere. Irrigation is the obvious solution to drought difficulties, yet it is banned in many European vineyards since wine-growers are not trusted to use the technique responsibly (it can damage quality by stimulating over-high yields). European wine-growers also know from experience that limited drought stress is good for wine quality. There is no remedy whatsoever for a cold summer or a wet harvest (though on occasion Christian Moueix of Château Pétrus in Pomerol has been known to use a hovering helicopter to dry vines and plastic sheeting to stop water penetrating the soil). Harvesting is ideally done by hand, with grapes being gathered whole and intact in small boxes, and all damaged fruit being discarded before crushing and pressing. Machine harvesting is also used to cut costs, and in hot regions to harvest in cool conditions during the night.

THE WINEMAKER

Once the grapes are grown and picked, the winemaker's role begins. What happens next depends on whether the grapes are red or white. Most white grapes have the juice pressed out of them and removed from the skins as soon as possible. Sometimes, however, a period of chilled skin contact follows to extract perfume and extra flavor from the skins, albeit at the risk of deepening color. Red grapes, by contrast, are merely crushed. They are then macerated so that the skins can surrender their vital color, flavor and texture elements to the must. In most cases, this corresponds with fermentation, though sometimes, especially for Pinot Noir-based wines, it precedes it. (Almost all red grapes, as it happens, have white juice; red wines are only red, purple, or black because the color has been soaked out of the skins and into the juice.) Pink wines spend a short time in contact with their skins, whereas rich, dense red wines intended for long aging often enjoy a good long soak with their skins even after fermentation has finished. (If the harvest has been rainy, incidentally, excess water can be extracted from grapes by freezing them, or removed from musts by techniques including vacuum evaporation and reverse osmosis.)

Fermentation is the fundamental principle of winemaking: it means the conversion of sugar to alcohol and carbon dioxide by the action of yeast. The winemaker has several decisions to make here, including the choice of fermentation temperature and the type of yeast used. Fresh, cool, crisp white wines need to be fermented slowly at a cool temperature; most red wines are fermented more quickly at warm or very warm temperatures, since this helps with extraction of color, flavor and texture from the skins. (Sometimes red wines may be fermented at relatively cool temperatures to increase fresh-fruit flavors.) Yeasts can either be cultured, in which case the type of flavor print they leave on the wine will be predictable; or fermentation can be left to wild yeasts: those which exist on grape skins, float on the air and are found in the winery itself. In this case, the flavors are likely to be more complex, but sometimes less predictable. If the grapes have insufficient sugar to produce well-balanced levels of alcohol, concentrated grape juice or sugar itself may be added to boost alcohol levels (this is common in cool climates). Powdered acid can also be added if the natural acidity in the grapes is felt to be deficient (this is common in hot climates).

Some red wines (like Beaujolais) taste especially soft, fruity and perfumed, their aroma often suggesting bananas. This effect is achieved by a technique called carbonic maceration. Here, whole bunches of grapes are placed in a sealed tank under a blanket of carbon dioxide, where they start to ferment spontaneously, without the action of yeast. A small amount of alcohol is produced, while plentiful aromatic compounds are extracted from the grapes. These grapes are then crushed and normal fermentation follows.

Another choice for the winemaker which affects flavor greatly is whether or not to use new oak. Makers of white wine have to make this choice well before the harvest, since the subtlest oaked white wines are always those which have actually fermented in new casks. (Fermenting a white wine in a stainless-steel tank, then running it into a new wooden cask after fermentation, gives an obvious hard, oaky taste.) Cask fermentation is harder to achieve for red wine since the wine needs to macerate with the skins, but once maceration

...a subtle creaminess, especially when the wine has fermented in new wood.

is over, many top-quality red wines are run into casks to conclude their fermentation. Simpler oaked flavors can be achieved by adding oak chips or staves to white or red wines as they ferment.

If a winemaker chooses to use large, old-oak casks (as are traditional, for example, in Germany) or stainless-steel tanks, he or she will be aiming to emphasize the clean, crisp, fruity flavors of the wine. Vessels of this sort have no impact on the wine's flavor, though a large old-oak cask can have a gently oxidative effect, rounding out the edges of the wine contained in it.

Yeast lees which fall from the wine during and after fermentation can also add flavor to a wine. Makers of white wine, in particular, find that leaving the new wine in contact with the lees for an extended period gives it a subtle creaminess, especially when the wine has fermented in new wood; the lees are sometimes stirred into the wine at regular intervals to increase this effect. Some wines (like the best Muscadets) are bottled directly off their lees to give an extra-fresh flavor. Winemakers are even experimenting with leaving red wines on their lees for an extended period. This is unusual, since red wines normally need to be racked (moved from barrel to barrel) to keep their freshness, develop flavor, aid clarification and avoid unpleasantly smelly reduction aromas and flavors. (Reduction is the opposite of oxidation: it is what happens when a wine has too little exposure to air.) Winemakers who want lees flavour in red wine (for extra richness and textural depth) therefore use a technique called micro-oxygenation, which involves injecting a tiny stream of oxygen bubbles through the wine at regular intervals to replace the racking process.

You may see a reference on back labels to

"malolactic fermentation", "malo", or "MLF". This is not a true fermentation at all, but a bacteriological conversion of malic acid into lactic acid and carbon dioxide. All red wines undergo this, but only some white wines. Its effect in the latter is to soften the balance and smooth out the flavor (since lactic acid is "milkier" than the appley malic acid), so for wines in which crisp, refreshing, fruity acid plays a leading role – like most German white wines, or crunchy, fruit-filled whites based on Sauvignon Blanc – winemakers tend to prevent the malolactic fermentation from happening. Rich Chardonnay wines, on the other hand, usually undergo total or partial malolactic fermentation to give them an extra softness.

The final decisions a winemaker has to make concern stabilization,
fining and filtration of the wine before bottling. The purpose of these processes is to make sure that the wine will not come to any harm once it's on the shelf – in other words, that it will not begin fermenting again, turn cloudy or throw an unwelcome deposit. For that reason, wines bottled young will usually be chilled (to precipitate tartrate crystals) and be both fined and filtered so that they are bright and deposit-free for the consumer. By contrast, wines bottled after some time spent in oak cask tend to be naturally bright and stable, and can actually be damaged by treatments of this sort, especially by fine-mesh filtrations. Sediment in well-stored, older fine red wines is almost always a positive and welcome sign that such wines have not been excessively fined, filtered and treated.

the taste of wine

FORTIFIED AND SPARKLING WINES

Before we leave the human role in winemaking, here is a brief description of how some special wine types are made.

Fortification means the addition of spirit to grape must or partially fermented wine to prevent or arrest fermentation, since yeasts cannot continue their activity in the presence of alcohol levels much over 15 percent by volume. Depending on the moment at which the wine is fortified, any natural sugar present remains in its sweet, unfermented state. When grape juice itself is fortified, the resulting drink (known in France as a *mistelle*) is very sweet; examples include Pineau des Charentes and Moscatel de Valencia. The most famous fortified wines (to which the spirit is added when part or wholly fermented) are sherry, port and Madeira (see the sections on Spain and Portugal in "Places" for details).

Sparkling wine can be made in several ways. The simplest method is to pump carbon dioxide into the wine, as one might pump air into a bicycle tyre; this method (called carbonation) is only used for the cheapest fizz. Every other sparkling wine acquires its bubbles from a second alcoholic fermentation. In this case, a little sugar and yeast are added to a fully fermented, dry wine in a closed container. As there is nowhere for the carbon dioxide gas produced by this second fermentation to go, it dissolves in the wine, emerging as foam when the pressure is relieved and the closed container opened. The easiest place for this second fermentation to take place is in a large tank, since the wine can be filtered before bottling, eliminating the sediment produced by the second fermentation; this simple method of making sparkling wine is called *cuve close* in French or the "Charmat process" elsewhere. All of the finest sparkling wines, however, undergo their sec-

the taste of wine

...the bottle is turned the right way up and uncapped, expelling the icy plug of sediment.

ond fermentation in bottle, ideally in cool, slow conditions, and they generally have an extended aging period during which the wine exchanges flavors with the yeasty lees. The sediment left by the second fermentation has to be removed, however, and one way of doing this is to decant the wine from one bottle into another, filtering it en route (this is called *transvasement* in French, or the transfer method in English; it is also that used for bottle-fermented Australian sparkling wines). The best method of all, however, is that used in Champagne and for the finest sparkling wine from other regions of the world, whereby the bottles are gradually up-ended (over a week or two using special *gyropalettes*) allowing the yeast sediment to slide slowly into the bottle's neck. The neck is then frozen, the bottle turned the right way up again and uncapped, expelling the icy plug of sediment. The wine is finally topped up and corked. This is known as the Champagne method or the *méthode traditionnelle* ('traditional method') – or, of course, the *méthode Champenoise* in Champagne itself.

route three: people

Most of us enjoy wine because of its variety. A fresh, grapey Moscato d'Asti is wine; so, too, is a black, explosive glass of young vintage port. This section celebrates that diversity. Dividing wines into styles allows us to swoop like swallows over the entire vinous landscape and make connections which the geographical approach leaves obscure. It is also useful, in that most of us want to buy a particular style of wine for dinner tonight rather than, say, something from the Rhône or Napa Valleys. A quick look into this section will provide some handy suggestions.

wine styles

"Au printemps," sang Jacques Brel in 1958, "au printemps, et mon coeur et ton coeur sont repeints au vin blanc... ". Brel's opening metaphor for spring, in a song unusually charged with vitality and optimism, saw "your heart and my heart repainted with white wine". I've never been able to forget those lines: they seem to sum up so well the pungency, shock and delight of a really bracing glass of white (as well as bright spring, of course, and love itself). It must have been Sauvignon Blanc, though, surely? Other varieties imply other moments, other songs. Here, we explore the full repertoire.

WHITE WINES

LIGHT AND MEDIUM-BODIED DRY WHITES

The driest, flintiest and sharpest of all dry white wines are produced in Europe. They include brisk, lemony Muscadet and its still tarter cousin Gros Plant du Pays Nantais; any still wine from the Champagne region; most wines of QbA, QmP and Kabinett status labeled "Trocken" or "Halbtrocken" from Germany; some of the great Sauvignon Blanc wines from the Loire (either varietally labeled, or sold as Sancerre, Pouilly-Fumé, Quincy, Reuilly and Menetou-Salon) as well as other Loire wines based on Chenin Blanc and labeled "Sec"; and some Chablis. You will also find most plain Bordeaux Sauvignon Blanc to be pungently dry, as is Jurançon Sec. True, Portuguese Vinho Verde fits this profile, with its appley slenderness and prickle of carbonation, though much of the Vinho Verde sold outside the country is deliberately sweetened for export. The wines of Spain's cool, rainy Galicia tend to be perfumed and elegantly, briskly dry, too.

There is an intriguing variety of flavors to be found within this category. Some wines (like Jurançon and Galician Albariño) can offer a spectrum of fruit flavors; some (like Sancerre, Pouilly-Fumé and Chablis) are stony, flinty or smoky, with occasional grassy notes; some (like Muscadet *sur lie*) show a charge of bready flavor from the lees.

This, in general, is not a style to which the grape-growing areas of the southern hemisphere are suited; even cool regions such as Australia's Tasmania, South Africa's Elgin or New Zealand's Marlborough receive generous sunlight, leading to wines with a combination (unusual in Europe) of relatively high alcohol and high acidity. This gives them more body, even though (especially from Tasmania) they may also be tart. In any case, the winemakers of newer wine-growing areas (most of whom are acutely market-focused) tend not to identify much demand for slender, sharp white wines among their customers. If Muscadet didn't already exist, they might argue, would anyone decide to invent it?

Now, I don't know your opinion of oysters, but if (like me) you relish them, then you will certainly understand why such wines exist. They are the perfect partner for the raw-iodine charge of a fresh oyster and its marine juices, as well as for other seafood and fish; they also make invigorating aperitif wines.

Medium-bodied dry whites constitute a much broader category. Let's begin with the least characterful of all good-quality medium-bodied dry whites: those from Italy. I don't want to imply that this is a failing. Anybody who drinks half a bottle or a bottle of wine with an evening meal will know that the best wines are not necessarily those which impress most at first sip. A bright, brash Australian white can taste superb for the first half-dozen mouthfuls, then may become a monotonous, crashing bore as you struggle to finish the rest of the bottle. Almost every wine in Italy, by contrast, is made to be drunk with food,

and top Frascati (with its delicate white-almond nuttiness) or Soave (with its soft, pear flavor) make exceptionally amenable and adaptable food partners. Other Italian wines in this category include dry Orvieto, supple and fruity Lugana, gently vegetal Gavi and the fresher, more lemony Verdicchio dei Castelli di Jesi (a fuller-bodied Italian version of Muscadet).

Most wine-producing countries throughout the world have their own equivalent of these wines: middle-of-the-road whites designed for drinking young with minimum fuss. Within France, much lesser white burgundy falls into this category, and many of these wines (like a well-made Mâcon-Villages) offer some of the best value from France. Gen-

erous in Chardonnay character without the distraction of lush oak, they rely on a discreet mesh of fruit, alcohol and vinosity for their bones and sinews.

Medium-bodied, plumply fruited white wines also form the core offering in Alsace, with grape varieties providing variations in style and weight of flavor. Riesling-based wines provide the driest, slenderest and most challenging choice, while Pinot Gris and Gewürztraminer often pass across into spicy, rich and full-bodied territory. Further south, many white wines produced in the Languedoc are, perhaps surprisingly, medium-bodied rather than full-bodied: the typical Chardonnay Vin de Pays d'Oc is a lighter, fresher and more elegant wine than the aver-

age California or Australian Chardonnay. Spain's Rueda, Somontano and Penedès whites are all medium-bodied; indeed, the Verdejo grape used in Rueda can be surprisingly sharp (its name alludes to its "greenness"). Portuguese whites produced from native varieties such as Fernão Pires or Encruzado (used, respectively, in Bairrada and Dão as well as for varietal wines from elsewhere) are usually medium-bodied but tend to be restrained, often with haunting scents, like those of wild flowers.

The majority of East European white wines are medium-bodied, both because the climates of Hungary, Bulgaria and Romania naturally produce wines of that style, and because the winemaking sophistication which trowels

They are the
perfect partner
for the raw-iodine charge of a fresh oyster and its marine juices, as well as for other seafood and fish.

extra layers of richness into white wines is not yet commercially viable there. Of the three, Hungary has proved the most well adapted to white-wine production; indeed, Hungarian whites vinified from some of its fine native grape varieties like Furmint and Hárslevelű (and picked at full ripeness) are among the most characterful medium-bodied whites you can buy inexpensively. Romanian whites are, in general, fatter and softer (and sometimes sweeter), while Bulgarian whites often lack the intrinsic complexity of flavor to be found in Hungary.

In North America, the nuanced, sometimes understated Pinot Gris and Chardonnay wines of Oregon are both naturally medium-bodied, whereas the sunnier conditions of Washington State yield much brighter, more vividly flavored whites, though without the sheer weight and dimensions that California's languid climate provides. Canada's dry white wines, too, are medium-bodied and relatively unpretentious in style, though always carefully crafted.

The great medium-bodied white wines of the southern hemisphere include many of those made from Sauvignon Blanc and Riesling, and white wines in general which are bottled (as many increasingly are) without any oak influence. Among the most successful of these are, of course, Sauvignon Blanc wines from New Zealand, not only from the Marlborough region but also from Hawke's Bay and other parts of the country: on acidity levels alone, you might consider them rivals to slender Muscadet or Sancerre, yet the prodigious sunlight of the southern hemisphere means that their fruit flavors are much richer and more tropical in style, and their alcohol levels can also be surprisingly high. Sauvignon Blanc from the cooler zones of South Africa can be just as successful as that from New Zealand, albeit less consistently so and in a different style. Here the fruit flavors are more delicate and supple, more orchard-like, and often better suited to barrel-fermentation techniques and the richer, creamier influence that brings. A few of New Zealand's richest Chardonnays from Hawke's Bay or Kumeu, near Auckland, might qualify as full-bodied, but most are medium-bodied, even when lavished with oak. These are sleek, refreshing, citric Chardonnays, full of fresh lemon and lime with a subtle lick of cream from oak and lees contact.

Australia's key medium-bodied whites include some of its Chardonnays from cooler-climate sites such as Tasmania (in which high acidity, both ripe and natural, makes for challenging drinking), the Mornington Peninsula and the Adelaide Hills. Many vineyards in these last two regions have been planted relatively recently, and a clear sense of stylistic direction has yet to emerge; yet the pure, limpid fruit flavors and natural delicacy of those made without oak bode well for the future.

Australian Riesling, too, comes into this category, although it tends not to be taken as seriously as Chardonnay. The best bottles, however, from both past and present, prove conclusively that this is one of the great white-wine styles of the southern hemisphere. Once again, fruit flavors are dominant and oak plays no role; yet in place of the grape, apple and peach notes of German Riesling you'll find more tropical fruit (lime, guava, mango) backed by alcohol levels which make these wines very food-friendly.

FULL-BODIED DRY WHITES

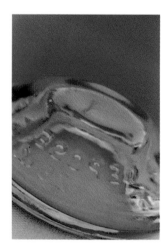

Most full-bodied dry white wines would, I suspect, be burgundy if they could. A great white burgundy from a good vintage, with around ten or fifteen years of cool cellar time behind it, is a magnificent drink: structured, nuanced, buttery, nutty, lemony, contriving to be both graceful yet masterful, and packed with allusive notes. The reason why lavishly oaked Chardonnay is so popular around the world is that it mimics the profile of well-aged white burgundy without necessarily having to go through the aging process first. Good burgundy needs age; in youth, it is inarticulate. Among the great white burgundy names are the Côte d'Or villages of Puligny-Montrachet, Chassagne-Montrachet and Meursault, with their attendant *premiers* and *grands crus*.

France's other full-bodied white wines include the best white Bordeaux from Pessac-Léognan and Graves. Like burgundy, these dry, oaked blends of Sémillon and Sauvignon Blanc also need time to ripen and unfold. In maturity, they are subtler and creamier than much white burgundy, with vegetal notes mixed in with soft apple and citrus fruit.

The Rhône Valley also produces wines of similar weight and subtlety, though with different aromas and flavors. Ordinary white Rhône is plump, low in acidity, with soft, muted, summer-fruit flavors. The best comes in three guises: white Hermitage, Crozes-Hermitage and St Joseph, where Marsanne and Roussanne provide (with age) sumptuous wines scented with white flowers; white Châteauneuf-du-Pape, based on a broader spectrum of varieties but also lush fat and syrupy; and finally Condrieu, based on Viognier, which with Alsace's Gewürztraminer is France's most aromatic white wine: profoundly floral, unctuous, heady and richly flavored. Uniquely among France's great white wines, it needs no aging.

What are the European rivals to these wines? White Rioja in Spain is one, though this tends to rely over-heavily on oak, while the Viura grape on which much white Rioja is based does not provide the subtly fruited complexity of French varieties. Both Spain and Italy, however, can produce fine oaked Chardonnay in regions such as Costers del Segre and Tuscany, respectively; in each case, these are probably the best full-bodied dry whites of each nation.

The most well-endowed wine producer in the northern hemisphere for full-bodied dry white wines is California; here, generous sunshine and long, regular growing seasons produce white wines high in alcohol and low in acidity, marked by ripe, summer-fruit flavors, and taking well to the generous caress of oak. Chardonnay, of course, is the most celebrated and widely grown variety, and even those from cooler areas like Carneros and the Russian River Valley often contain more than 14 percent alcohol by volume and show lush, rich characters, with peachy fruit weighed down by oak and lees notes.

Viognier is on the increase in California, too, and produces sumptuous, alcoholic, weighty wines marked by exotic floral scents such as gardenia. Indeed, the natural wealth of flavor of California's best dry whites (Sauvignon Blanc is less consistently successful here) means that some taste almost sweet. This touch of residual sugar is deliberately contrived by producers of inexpensive, branded white wines.

Apart from New Zealand and

A great white burgundy
from a good vintage... is a magnificent drink:
structured, nuanced, buttery, lemony,
contriving to be both
graceful yet masterful, too.

Australia's far south, most southern-hemisphere wine regions are, like California, naturally gifted for full-bodied, dry white wines. Chile's Chardonnays, for example, are almost always full-bodied and sweet-fruited, with generous alcohol levels and often a custard-like oak-and-lees influence, either from barrel-fermentation or from the use of oak chips and lees stirring in fermentation. Even Chardonnay from the cool Casablanca Valley is fundamentally full-bodied, despite its citric style of fruit. Argentina, too, tends to produce broad-beamed, chewy Chardonnays and other whites (including the local specialty Torrontés); only in Río Negro does a fresh, vivid edge creep into these.

There is more stylistic variation in South Africa, and more appreciation, too, of elegance and restraint, yet Chardonnay tends to be grown in warm sites, providing big-boned wines of pure flavor with a lighter lees influence than that common in California and Chile. Limestone soils and coastal climates help create complexity of flavor in areas such as Stellenbosch, Hermanus and Robertson, though the producer's own winemaking ambitions remain the most important factor.

Australia is famous for its full-bodied, canary-yellow wines, lavished with all the richness the country's generally hot climate and tradition of proficient winemaking can provide. Top-priced wines come from low-yielding vineyards with an emerging pedigree, and enjoy luxurious barrel-fermentation and aging; less expensive wines are marked simply by the sunny, melon-and-peach fruit typical of Australia, and are given a little inexpensive oak character by the use of toasty wood chips during the fermentation process.

There are also established regional traditions, providing different styles of full-bodied, dry whites. The Chardonnay and Semillon wines of the Hunter Valley, for example, have pollen-like, honeyed or toasty aromas and rich, chewy, complex flavors. Cowra, Padthaway and McLaren Vale all produce straightforward Chardonnay of exuberant style; Barossa Valley Chardonnay and Semillon has a decidedly lemony, salty note, while Chardonnay from the Eden Valley and Clare Valley is slightly fresher. Adelaide Hills Chardonnay is subtle and intricate, while Margaret River Chardonnay can be the most complex of all, with striking intensity of flavor and multi-layered notes from barrel-fermentation and aging. Other full-bodied dry whites are produced in Australia from Verdelho (often fermented without oak to emphasize its juicy, tropical-fruit character), Marsanne (rich, overt and mango-fruited) and Viognier (glycerous, heady and with a hauntingly floral character). Oaked styles of Australian Sauvignon Blanc also tend to be full-bodied; Coonawarra's can be richly asparagussy.

AROMATIC AND MEDIUM-DRY WHITES

Those who know wine cherish its aromas; this category is decidedly wine's perfumed garden. The white styles we've looked at so far include all the great food whites; here, we look at wines which are ideally suited to enjoying on their own, either as an aperitif or set aside from food altogether, to while away an afternoon among friends.

The great masters of this wine style are the Germans. Sipping a fine German wine, with its intense perfumes, low alcohol content and finely balanced, pure fruit flavors is an experience akin to listening to music or reading a poem: the pleasure seems more intellectual than physical. Most classical German wines are medium-dry in style. Historically, juice from late-ripening Riesling was rarely able to ferment to absolute dryness before winter threw a chill over the cellars, arresting fermentation; in any case, in wines like these in which alcohol plays such a submissive role, some sugar is needed to bring the high acidity into balance. In Germany, fully dry wines can

taste forced, especially from regions like the Mosel, Saar and Ruwer, where the climate naturally creates wines of absolute delicacy (dry wines from Baden and Franconia are fuller and better balanced). Among German medium-dry styles, there are subregional differences: the Mosel is characterized by flowery or mineral scents, apple and grape notes and zingy acidity; the Rheingau and the Nahe tend towards a pure summer-fruit style; Rheinhessen and the Pfalz are generally richer, softer and spicier.

Cross into France, and the aromatic theme is triumphantly maintained in Alsace. Gewürztraminer, with its exotic scents of litchi nuts, spices, cold cream and rose petals, is one of the world's most powerfully and arrestingly aromatic wines; Riesling, Pinot Gris and Muscat from Alsace can also be intensely aromatic. In general, those Alsace wines not described as either *vendange tardive* (late harvest) or *sélection des grains nobles* (a selection of botrytis-affected grapes) are dry; yet

Gewürztraminer and Pinot Gris, in particular, are both low-acid grape varieties which, when ripe, tend to produce off-dry or even medium-dry wines, though labels generally fail to mention this.

Across in the Loire Valley, Chenin Blanc-based wines are made in a medium-dry style (both *demi-sec* and *moelleux* are terms used for such wines, with the latter slightly sweeter than the former) in appellations such as Coteaux du Layon, Montlouis or Quarts de Chaume. These wines are marked by scents of damp hay, honeycomb, wax and orchard fruits. We'll take a look at the fully sweet wines of France later (see pages 122-125), but before we leave French borders, it's worth noting that the Viognier-based wines of Condrieu, already covered in the last section on full-bodied dry white wines, are also astonishingly aromatic – and some growers are beginning to harvest their Viognier grapes so late that the wines produced are rich and palpably sweet-edged in style.

Elsewhere in Europe, aromatic and medium-dry styles are less

common: the warmer climatic conditions found further south mean that fully dry or fully sweet styles are the norm. The delicate white wines of Spain's Galicia tend to be aromatic, although almost all are dry; Italy, too, has a small number of such *abboccato* (semi-dry) wines. Austria mimics Germany's system of *Prädikat* categories such as Kabinett, Spätlese and Auslese, but higher must weights are specified. This means that if the wines remain in medium-sweet or sweet styles, they tend to be richer than wines sold under the same descriptions in Germany; if dry, they have more structure and alcoholic backbone.

Some Hungarian Tokáji is made in medium-dry style: here the terms to look out for are Szamorodni Edes, Aszú three-puttonyos, or Aszú four-puttonyos as well as the newer category of Late Harvest (Késői Szüretelésű) wines. Hungary also produces a variety of aromatic, dry whites, made from obscure but useful crossings like Irsai Oliver, Zenit and Cserszegi Fűszeres.

Throughout the rest of the wine world, medium-dry wines tend to be designed to exploit commercial opportunities rather than express a sense of sensual uniqueness or sense of place: Australia's Yellow Tail brand, for example, owes much of its popularity in the USA to its high residual sugar levels, and pink Blush Zinfandel is tellingly sweet, too. Wines made from aromatic grape varieties like Gewürztraminer enjoy modest success in most southern-hemisphere wine-producing countries, though the best of these (from Casa Marín in Chile or Villa Maria in New Zealand) are now made in an almost-dry style. Aromatic Muscat is generally made in either a dry or sweet style, but is rarely medium-dry (the Orange Muscat and Flora blend produced by Australia's Brown Brothers is an exception). One of the few "native" aromatic varieties found in the southern hemisphere is Argentina's Torrontés: it is easy to mistake this spicy, musky, dry, alcoholic white for a Muscat, though its crisp acidity is often somewhat higher.

White wine, for me, implies a special moment: summer, oysters, the early stages of a lavish dinner. Red wine, on my drinking map, surrounds white as the ocean surrounds islands. Red wine is always first choice; red wine, in the end, *is* wine. It's what I like to drink every day, what I like to drink on Sundays, and what I like to drink on Christmas Day, too. Fortunately, there are "red" wines for every moment, from smooth-textured rose-reds to thick-textured coal-black wines. One of the greatest pleasures of my life has been exploring them, and I hope the following pages will inspire you to make discoveries of your own.

RED WINES

Red wines differ from whites: they possess an extra dimension. White wines are fermented from pressed juice alone; reds, as we learned in the first part of this book, contain color, flavor and textural matter extracted from grape skins. (The dry residue formed when wines are boiled away to nothing for analysis is known, by the way, as "extract", which is why chewy, heavy reds are described as "extractive".)

It's easy to praise a red wine by its color, depth and extract. It's easy to judge wines as if one were predicting the outcome of a brawl: the darker, more thickly textured and powerful the wine, the more likely that it will prove to be a winner. I've reached such conclusions; most of us have. Yet they're misguided.

I met a friend recently, one whom I hadn't seen for some months, for a drink. We had much to discuss. An initial beer gave way to wine. The red we chose was light in color and smooth in texture, with appetizing scents of raspberry and tar. Although it was served a little too warm, this bottle of Moulin-à-Vent (from France's Beaujolais region) was perfect for our conversation

without food. A chewy red would have made far less pleasurable drinking that summer evening. Light reds have a role.

Most of the world's naturally light red wines are grown in northern Europe, and are often made from the Pinot Noir grape variety. In regions such as France's Alsace or Jura, Germany's Ahr or Baden, or in Switzerland, this grape produces often pale-colored wines, with light tannins. As with Beaujolais (made from Gamay), these reds have the texture of a white wine, yet the curranty perfumes and flavors of a red; they are delicious chilled. Some Cabernet Franc-based reds from the Loire Valley can be similar (though they are usually darker in color than Pinot-based wines): names to look out for include Saumur-Champigny, Chinon and Bourgueil. Any red wine from Italy's Alto Adige or Germany's Württemberg made from the Trollinger grape (also known as the Schiava or Vernatsch) will be very pale, almost a rosé; the Jura's Poulsard grape, too, produces reds that are naturally lighter in color than many hot-climate rosé wines. Other Italian light red

wines include the vivaciously cherry-scented Valpolicella and Bardolino. Hungary's red wines also tend to be light, pale, soft-textured and tart, best chilled for maximum refreshment value.

Perhaps the oddest light red wine in existence is red Vinho Verde from Portugal. It sounds self-contradictory, I know, but red "green wine" does exist. To look at, you'd think it heavy rather than light, since it's often very dark in color. Yet it tastes slender and piercing, like acidic ink. It's an acquired taste to drink on its own, certainly, but with the grilled local sardines fished in abundance off Portugal's Atlantic coast, it makes memorably strange sense.

The medium-bodied category for red wines embraces a huge variety. Plenty more Pinot Noir-based reds, including almost all truly great red burgundies, fall into this category; indeed, one of the defining qualities of fine red burgundy is its ability to taste more profound and multi-dimensioned than a simple assessment of texture, flavor and depth would suggest. These wines acquire smoothness faster than most reds; yet

LIGHT AND MEDIUM-BODIED REDS

the aromas and flavors (of fruits such as cherry, raspberry and plum) seem to broaden and modulate into something deeply complex, savory, meaty or even fiery with age. The best red varietal Pinot Noir (from California, Oregon, Tasmania and from New Zealand's Martinborough, Marlborough and Central Otago regions) increasingly mimics this powerful, referential grace.

Just as burgundy straddles the line between light and medium-bodied, so claret (red Bordeaux) straddles the line between medium-bodied and full-bodied. Moreover, in this maritime region prone to changeable harvest weather, a vintage can make all the difference: very little red Bordeaux was truly medium-bodied in 2000 or 2003, whereas almost all red Bordeaux was medium-bodied in 1997 and 2002. In general, it is true to say that the less expensive and less "serious" Bordeaux tends to be medium-bodied, whereas great Bordeaux is usually full-bodied, certainly in its youth. Subregions can also affect this equation. Within the Médoc, for example, Margaux tends to be medium-bodied and Pauillac full-bodied; and reds from the smaller appellations like Bourg, Blaye, Graves de Vayres, Premières Côtes de Bordeaux and Bordeaux itself will normally be medium-bodied. This need not carry derogatory quality connotations: a medium-bodied Bordeaux is often a wine of ample blackberry elegance, complexity and gently cedary refinement. Indeed, few wines produced elsewhere in the world can match its light-footed, supremely digestible, perfectly balanced style.

Do Bordeaux-style blends from California and elsewhere in North America succeed in imitating it? Very rarely. Almost all red wines from California made from

light and medium-bodied reds

Few wines produced elsewhere in the world can match
Bordeaux's light-footed,
supremely digestible,
perfectly balanced style.

grapes which achieve complete ripeness will emerge in the full-bodied zone, though some big-brand blends can be medium-bodied by default – they simply lack intensity, impact and definition of flavor. A truer, lighter balance with full ripeness is usually achieved in the Merlot and Cabernet Sauvignon wines of Long Island.

Many of the wines of France's northern Rhône Valley are thought to be full-bodied but are, in fact, more commonly medium-bodied. The Syrah grape grown in the mainly granitic soil of the northern Rhône yields vigorous and vivacious red wines of considerable perfume, yet acidity levels remain high and the lesser wines of the region (such as Crozes-Hermitage or St Joseph) can often lack extract after a difficult year. Côte-Rôtie, too, is rarely more than medium-bodied (it often contains an admixture of white Viognier grapes), though its enticing and extensive range of aromas, thrilling vigor and the creamy poise of its flavors lend it unquestioned grandeur. Most well-made southern Rhône reds (for example Châteauneuf-du-Pape) will be full-bodied, but the reds of some adjacent appellations (such as Coteaux du Tricastin) can be more slender; as can the herby yet restrained reds of the larger Provence appellations like Côtes du Ventoux, Côtes du Lubéron and Côtes de Provence itself.

Other French medium-bodied reds include regional specialties such as the peppery Côtes du Frontonnais and the slightly deeper, more minerally Côtes du Saint-Mont. Bergerac and Buzet both tend to be medium-bodied, with some of the fresh, cassis flavor of Bordeaux.

Italy has a large variety of medium-bodied red wines, often with relatively high acidity and some pleasingly bitter backnotes; such wines make exceptionally good food partners, especially for pasta dishes. Barbera, for example, can often be one of the most pungently characterful of all medium-bodied reds, with lots of raspberry or plum perfume and flavor, always given a fine, slicing edge by juicy acidity; its tannin levels are variable. Piedmont's lighter Nebbiolo wines, too, are medium-bodied, with relatively pale colors, fragrant scents, tart yet complex flavors and a compellingly dry, tannin-dusted finish. The reds of Trentino and Friuli, even those supposedly made from "bigger" red grape varieties such as Cabernet Sauvignon, are rarely produced with low enough yields or ripe enough fruit to achieve a full-bodied density of flavor; the best come from the Colli Orientali. The deepest forms of dry Valpolicella – such as the kernel-flavored Ripasso and heady yet graceful Amarone – both fall into this category.

You could call Tuscany "Italy's Bordeaux" (just as Piedmont is its "Burgundy") as the Sangiovese-based wines of the region share something of Bordeaux's vintage-dependent dual nature. While the best wines from the hottest years are unquestionably full-bodied, more ordinary Chianti is a medium-bodied wine (and the thinnest is decidedly light). Like Bordeaux, too, ordinary Chianti can be a thoroughly satisfying, well-balanced wine for food, its relatively prominent acidity providing freshness and liveliness, and its subtle flavors of apple, plum, coffee and laurel combine well with the typical Italian food flavors of olive oil, herbs, tomato and well-seasoned meats.

In contrast to those of Italy, Spain and Portugal's red wines tend to be built along sturdy, full-bodied lines, even though they can on occasion be pale in color with soft, recessive tannins. A sweet-scented, well-aged Rioja or Valdepeñas, for example, is fairly smooth and easy to drink, though the overall impression is one of supple and sometimes succulent richness.

Few Eastern European reds are as yet made with low enough yields, from ripe enough fruit and with adequately extractive winemaking to qualify as more than medium-bodied. The best are, at present, simple and friendly red wines built around plain fruit flavors often melded

and softened by a period of pre-bottle aging.

Europe's often cloudy skies and unpredictable climate patterns make it the natural home of the medium-bodied red; not so the wine-producing countries of the southern hemisphere. The clearer light, brighter sunshine and generally hot, desert-like wine-growing environments of Chile, Argentina, South Africa and Australia mean that the majority of reds in these countries are built on a bigger scale than the average Bergerac, Chianti or Bulgarian Merlot. The chief exceptions are Pinot Noir-based reds, mentioned above, grown in the cooler-climate regions of Victoria, South Australia and Tasmania.

As well as, of course, the Cabernet- and Merlot-based reds of New Zealand. These are naturally medium-bodied, even though their colors may be dark; their fundamental balance is not dissimilar to the red Cabernet Franc-based wines of the Loire, with often vivid acidity underpinning brisk fruit and moderate tannin levels. Achieving full ripeness can be a problem; less successful examples have a green, herbaceous streak to them. The best of these lively wines, however, make invigorating drinking, and seem to acquire aged characteristics (leather and tobacco, for example) more easily than many other southern-hemisphere reds.

light and medium-bodied reds

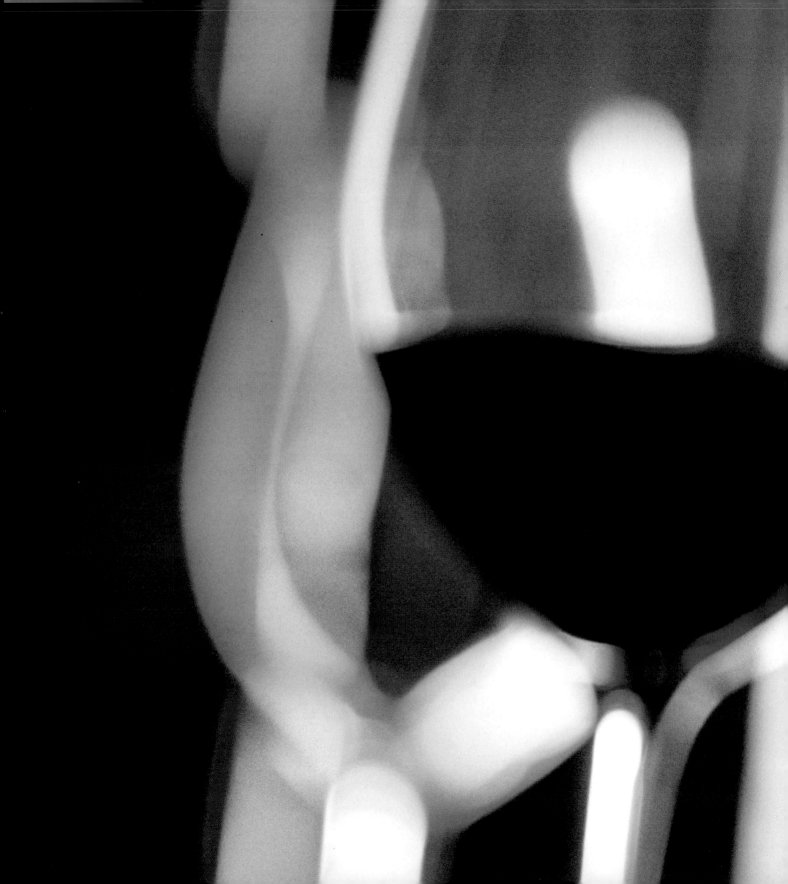

FULL-
BODIED
REDS

Most wine-drinkers begin by preferring white wine to red; most soon come to appreciate both, and most end up enjoying red wine above all, and the fuller-bodied the better. Drinkers in wine-producing countries such as France, Italy or Spain overwhelmingly favor red wine over white, and have done so for centuries. Red wine delivers more to the drinker (since it contains extracts white wines don't), and red wine in general accompanies food more rewardingly and engagingly than white. The perceived health benefits of red wine have added further to its popularity. Full-bodied reds, therefore, are the key wine style for many drinkers.

This puts certain countries at a disadvantage. You'll seldom drink a truly full-bodied red from Germany, Switzerland, Austria, Hungary or New Zealand. They exist, but they're uncommon, and are the outcome of an exceptionally warm season and an assiduous grape-grower. France itself, surprisingly enough, does not produce full-bodied reds with ease; only the southern half of the country is regularly warm enough, and even then harvest rains can wash potentially full-bodied wines back into medium-bodied dilution. Historical misconceptions play a part, too: many drinkers, for example, still casually think of red burgundy as a hearty, full-bodied wine. Insofar as this was ever the case, it was based on the blended burgundies of the pre-1980 period which often contained "medicinal" wines from North Africa, the Languedoc or the Rhône Valley. True red burgundy, even the most profound, is rarely more than medium-bodied. Some producers, admittedly, create heavily extracted, inky red burgundy, yet such wines generally lack balance, finesse and conviction, and age awkwardly.

Full-bodied red Bordeaux, by contrast, is a much more regular occurrence, chiefly by benefit of vintage. Generous, hot years in Bordeaux (such as 1990, 2000 and 2005) produce full-bodied reds right across the quality spectrum, down to and including what are called the *petit château* wines: wines from the many thousands of small properties powdering the region. The best wines in most average-to-good vintages (years like 1985, 1986, 1995, 1996 and 2001) are most accurately described as full-bodied, too. In Bordeaux, this means a wine of ample, even prolific tannin (the best Bordeaux needs aging for a decade or more to give that clenched grip time to open and soften) and intense yet often vivid fruit characteristics. Although many regions use more new oak than traditional wine producers do in Bordeaux, the refined, cedar-and-pencil scent of French oak barrels seems to infuse and saturate the sensual personality of the wine more thoroughly here than anywhere else. Meaty, spicy characters are common in Merlot-based Bordeaux from regions such as St Emilion and Pomerol, and here, too, the wines seem to possess the most cream, most fat, most richness. Cabernet Sauvignon-based Bordeaux (from the Médoc and Pessac-Léognan) rarely has that fat, rounded quality; instead, there is a sense of restrained voluptuousness, of textured depth, of refined and sometimes driving concentration. Cassis and mulberry flavors are typical of a young Médoc and of Pessac-Léognan.

The third of France's great red-wine areas, the Rhône Valley, is another transition zone in which you will find light, medium-bodied and full-bodied red wines. Despite their reputation, the classic wines of the northern Rhône are rarely full-bodied; only the appellations of Hermitage itself, the best Crozes-Hermitage from hot vintages, and Cornas have the muscle and structure to qualify. Even then, it is by virtue of concentration of perfume, spice and extract meshed into vivid, often high-

acid fruit, that they do so; they are rarely fat, lush and softly full-bodied. For that style, you have to push on south to Châteauneuf-du-Pape. The best of these memorably named wines are amiable and accessible, with an almost soupy, lazily full-bodied style and sweet-edged, blackberry character. Good Châteauneuf matures slowly to a savory old age. The most skillful producers of lesser southern Rhône wines (like Lirac, Gigondas, Vacqueyras, Costières de Nîmes and Côtes du Rhône-Villages) can make smaller wines of the same style in most years.

Red wines from Provence, the Languedoc and southwest France certainly have the climatic potential to be full-bodied, and the best of them are. Bandol and Coteaux d'Aix-en-Provence-les Baux can be earthy, richly textured wines with the flavors of herbs and black olives; there are more herbs, too, alongside fiery, stony flavors in the darker wines of Coteaux du Languedoc, Corbières and Minervois. Madiran is tougher still (it needs a rich, meaty stew, and 12 hours' decanting, to open it up fully) and has a more mineral-laden style, as does Cahors.

The most ambitious vins de pays, made from varieties including Syrah, Merlot, Mourvèdre and Cabernet, can all be full-bodied.

Like France, Italy is more uniformly suited to producing light or medium-bodied reds than truly full-bodied ones. The exceptions are the country's greatest red wines after good or outstanding vintages: Barolo, Barbaresco, Amarone, Chianti Classico and Brunello di Montalcino in the north, and Montepulciano d'Abruzzo, Salice Salentino and Taurasi in the south. Wines made outside the traditional DOC or DOCG framework, and often from "international" rather than Italian grape varieties, can be just as full-bodied: the celebrated Sassicaia and Ornellaia wines from Bolgheri are just two examples, and many more can be found within Piedmont and in central Tuscany.

Flavors? The Italian understanding of "full-bodied" is, in terms of balance, not dissimilar to what you'll find in the biggest wines of the northern Rhône. In other words, these are not fat, sweet, alcoholically rich wines which slide with unction over the tongue. Instead, they retain great power and intensity, often with high acidity levels, yet combine all this with ample tannin and extract to create perfumed, close-knit and sometimes challenging wines designed for long cellar storage. Over time, they

wine styles

soften and unfold, revealing their secrets, yet never actually become either soft or easy. Aromas and flavors you may find in them in youth include red and black fruits, especially cherry and plum, with licorice and cloves, apple, coffee, tar, and floral scents of violet or rose. Since this is Italy, and since Italians love bitter flavors, there will often be a refreshing bitter or bittersweet edge to the fruit. With time, the wines become more savory, with hints of cigar leaf, fine leather and warm earth. Wines from the south, such as Salice Salentino, Taurasi or Sicily's best reds (like Regaleali's Rosso del Conte or Corvo's Duca Enrico), may well have sweeter styles of fruit, a plumper profile, and be slightly more accessible in their youth than the northern classics, yet they still retain Italy's hallmark vividness and vitality at their core. Full-bodied non-traditional reds such as Sassicaia will combine an expressive varietal character with often lavish oak influence, yet once again Italy's general liveliness and briskness will color their fruit.

In contrast to Italy and France, Spain's natural vocation is for full-bodied reds, though the country has only recently acquired the confidence to make and offer these to the world without taming – and sometimes emasculating – them in wood over many years first. That

"wood-tamed" style of full-bodied red, of course, remains popular: most famously from Rioja, but also from less celebrated regions like Valdepeñas. New-wave Riojas, many of them from single-vineyard sites, tend not to have the tissue-like softness of these classic, old-style, well-aged wines; instead, the typical strawberry/plum fruit of Tempranillo from Rioja is given greater vigor and density, shaped by the tannins and perfumes of new-oak barrels. Today, these are less likely to be American (hence sweet and vanillic) than they have been in the past, and are more likely to be French (with a toastier, spicier style). You'll find a similar dual approach to full-bodied reds in Navarra.

The key new name in full-bodied Spanish reds is Ribera del Duero. The cool nights and hot days of this upland region give its Tempranillo-based wines a punchier and more rumpled, textured style than in Rioja, with plum notes taking over from strawberry in its fruit; oak is often lavishly used, adding further to the powerhouse style. Nearby Toro is just as hot but lacks the cooler nights; its wines are no less full-bodied and plummy, but tend to have softer tannins. Increasingly important regions of inland Spain for richly alcoholic, often tarry reds of deep plum/blackberry fruit include Cariñena, Calatayud and Jumilla: great value for a

winter's night. Priorato, finally, is most decidedly full-bodied when at its best (though this semi-mountainous region can also produce lighter, more tenuous wines if the vineyards are located low on shaded valley floors). Look for an exotic, multi-faceted and sometimes medicinal range of aromas and flavors packed around spicy-sweet Garnacha-based fruit.

Portugal's most full-bodied reds come, with seeming paradox, from each end of the country. The port-producing region of the Douro is capable of rich reds with complex fruit characters based on a mix of classic port-grape varieties; the southerly Alentejo region, too, can produce deep reds of softer fruit and sweeter character. The reds of Bairrada and Dão often have a tighter and more acidic style, with tough, middleweight fruit.

Moving to southeastern Europe, Bulgaria and Romania have the potential to make soft and gratifyingly full-bodied young reds; indeed, British wine-buyers worked hard to unearth such wines over the 1990s. It was relatively easy to change the traditional approach to long cellar aging, but much harder to find top-quality vineyards to provide the healthy, ripe red grapes such wines demand. They remain uncommon. In Greece, by contrast, the medium-bodied, sometimes tired or raisiny red wines of tradition have given way to a range of deeper, fresher-flavored wines from hard-working small-scale producers. Traditional producers, too, have taken old styles and updated them to provide wines without great color or tannin, yet with ample fruit and expressive, savory, wild-herb flavors.

It's when you leave Europe altogether, however, that full-bodied red wines become the norm; this is just one reason behind the success of wine-growing countries such as Chile, Argentina or Australia. Yet you don't have to abandon the northern hemisphere to find the kind of wine-growing environments that can deliver dark, sturdy, amply fleshed red wines with easygoing regularity: northern and central California can certainly do this. Once clear of the fog-prone coastal districts, the long Californian summer and its generous sunshine encourage wines of enormous girth and alcoholic power, built around an impressive core of soft yet peppery berry fruit. Oak adds extra layers, as does cellar time: the end result is that complex aromas and flavors (of tobacco, tree resins, turned earth) are

built into the fruit, which itself softens further in bottle. Napa is the best-known region for red wines (particularly Cabernet Sauvignon) of these extravagant dimensions, yet many other districts can produce wines with the same overall shape and weight. Other grape varieties used for full-bodied wines include sweet-fruited, alcoholic, softly tannic Zinfandel, powerful and stewy Petite Sirah and Charbono, savory Syrah and sometimes succulent, sometimes brusquely inarticulate Merlot. The Merlots of Washington State are no less full-bodied, but are often darker in color with greater freshness and pungency, melding more harmoniously with their oak; Cabernet Sauvignon from Washington can be resoundingly deep and ripe.

The bright light and prolific sunshine of southern-hemisphere viticultural environments is perfect for providing winemakers with the fruit needed for generously full-bodied red wines. Argentina, Chile, South Africa and Australia all became major suppliers of inexpensive, full-bodied reds to the world's wine-drinkers during the 1990s; the

more carefully crafted, expensive reds of these countries are also growing in variety and popularity. The differences between them are emphasis and style: Chile tends to produce reds of soft, rounded, supple, juicy fruit, while Argentina's are more tannic, savory and extractive. Australia's have bright, limpid fruit characters and a clean style, often with the sweet sheen of oak. Those of South Africa are more varied: some can be tough and charmless; others have a richly fruited, vividly balanced style; the best are pungent, tight, almost roasted.

There are many other differences, too, depending chiefly on grape variety, climate and wine-making styles rather than (as in Europe) soil and microclimate. In Chile, for example, reds from the Casablanca Valley, San Antonio or Leyda have a decidedly fresher balance and more curranty style of fruit than those from the other, warmer zones of the country. Cabernet Sauvignon and Merlot both produce deliciously accessible full-bodied reds; this is even true of the country's finest, most expensive wines, which may be marked by the

sweet perfume and rich texture of expensive oak-cask aging, but which nonetheless rarely have anything tough or even firm about them. No country produces more easy-drinking full-bodied red wine than Chile.

Argentina is a contrast. Its beefiest, blackest wines come from Mendoza's classic sub-regions such as Luján de Cuyo and Maipu and tend to be made from Malbec, though Cabernet Sauvignon, Merlot, Syrah, Tannat, Sangiovese, Tempranillo and Bonarda are also used. The best of these are almost somber wines, often with hard-hitting tannins and generous helpings of earthy, mineral flavors. Full-bodied reds from Cafayate in the north can be just as dense, but with more incisive fruit and less abrasive tannins; while those from Río Negro (in particular Merlot) have greater suppleness and poise.

Within South Africa, the differences are very much based on winemaking aspiration, though coastal regions such as Constantia, Elgin, Walker Bay or the Darling Hills can provide a fresher, slightly crisper style for climatic reasons. Cabernet Sauvignon and

Pinotage from classic, well-resourced and ambitious estates in areas such as Stellenbosch will regularly be amply oaked, richly textured and have resonant, fine-grained fruit flavors. Producers in Tulbagh, Wellington and Malmesbury have made a more recent specialism in varieties such as Syrah, Grenache and Mourvèdre, giving soft, voluptuous reds of savory, spicy style.

Australia produces a plethora of full-bodied reds. Biggest of all, perhaps, are the country's grand Shiraz wines from warmer areas such as the Barossa Valley or McLaren Vale: these are gutsy, salty, almost molasses-like on occasion, with thick blackberry fruit, high alcohol, soft tannins, fragrant sweet oak and variable acidity levels depending on the winemaker's approach. Some may even have a little unfermented sugar left in them, increasing the "porty" impression they leave. Australian Grenache is rarely as deep in color or as richly textured as Shiraz, but may rival it for sweet-fruited power. Cabernet Sauvignon can be very dark; it can also be much more briskly and freshly fruited, with bright, blackberry flavors, firm tannins and lots of black-pepper depth; Coonawarra is the key area for wines of this style. Look out, too, for wines from varieties such as Mourvèdre (Mataro) and Merlot, and for multi-variety blends; all these play variations on the full-bodied theme.

full-bodied reds

ROSÉ WINES

This is wine's light-entertainment division. We've all enjoyed a few great white wines and a few great red wines, but great rosé? It doesn't seem to exist. France offers one or two expensive pink wines from tiny appellations like Cassis and Bellet, but their prices have more to do with rarity than quality.

Why is pink wine never great? Partly because it is never expected to be. If a grower in Montrachet, Pauillac or Hermitage could be persuaded to try making the greatest rosé the world has ever known, on favorable wine-growing soil from old vines with low yields, then the rosé-of-rosés might emerge. But no one wants to pay much for pink wine, so it doesn't happen. It remains a cheap option.

Nothing wrong with that, of course, and there's still plenty of variety within the style as a whole. Many of the deepest rosé wines you can find come from Australia, made from Grenache or Shiraz: these plum-pink wines are knocking on the door of red wine, and their ample, juicy fruit flavors make them ideal for outdoor, barbecue drinking. When South Africa, Chile and Argentina think about making pink wine, this is generally the style they go for, too. The great hazard of rosé is that many consumers expect it to be off-dry or medium-sweet (thanks to a long legacy of highly commercial rosés such as Mateus, Lancers and Rosé d'Anjou).

France and Spain are the sources of the world's most interesting dry rosé, and Grenache (or Garnacha) is, as in Australia, frequently the grape used to make these. Rosé from Rioja and Navarra is usually an excellent buy, with a deep color, plenty of alcoholic backbone, roundly dry fruit flavors and an often peppery finish. The orange-hued rosés of the southern Rhône Valley in France (such as Lirac and Tavel) are not dissimilar: forceful and heady. The dry rosé wines of Provence are often pretty, with lighter, sometimes salmon-pink or even metallic pink tints, and a curvy, flirtatious bottle; in flavor terms, however, they can take neutrality to excess. The rosé wine of Bandol, by contrast, can be deep and structured.

Bordeaux produces some of the finest rosé money can buy, often as a by-product of red-winemaking: to concentrate the flavor of a red wine, a winemaker might "bleed" off some juice early on in the proceedings. This *rosé de saignée* ("bled pink") significantly and pleasingly echoes the quality of the Cabernet or Merlot-based red being made at the time. Bordeaux also has an official rosé appellation called Clairet, a term recalling the historical origin of the British synonym for red Bordeaux, claret. Burgundy, too, produces vivid rosé, though in tiny quantities: Marsannay is the name to look out for.

Scattered around France are various red-grape varieties which tend to produce such pale reds that you might almost think of them as rosé: Négrette in the Côtes du Frontonnais, Poulsard in the Jura, Gamay in Beaujolais and elsewhere, and Pinot Noir in areas such as Alsace, Champagne (for piercing, still red-pinks like Bouzy and Rosé de Riceys), Chablis (Irancy) and the Upper Loire. These can be memorable, but can also be sharp and challenging. The Loire in general is capable of producing excellent rosé; the popularity of the sweet, slushy Rosé d'Anjou, however, means that pungent, incisive, dry Loire rosés are hard to find, at least on export markets.

...these plum-pink wines are knocking on the door of red wine and their ample, juicy fruit flavors make them ideal for outdoor drinking.

The world of sparkling wines is, seemingly, more fixed and stable than that of other wine styles. There are fewer names to log into your cerebral wine file; vintages wreak less havoc on the pedigree of past performance. Why? The dominance of Champagne as sparkling wine's top dog is one reason; so, too, is the fact that sparkling-wine production requires considerable investment in equipment, storage, stock and marketing, making it less well-suited than other wines to small-grower participation.

That doesn't, however, mean that sparkling wines as a whole lack variety. The main stylistic poles are based on climatic variations: cool, even chilly conditions (like those in Champagne, Tasmania or fog-prone coastal valleys in California) produce crisp-edged sparkling wines of finesse and depth; whereas warmer conditions (like those of Catalonia in Spain or the Riverland in Australia) produce sparkling wines of a softer, rounder, easier style. There are cost implications, too: cool climates mean grapes which are more difficult to grow and wines which need longer storage time before sale. In general, then, the most expensive (and best) sparkling wines come from cool climates, and the cheaper (and less ambitious) sparkling wines come from warm climates.

Let's put a bit more flesh on these bare bones. You can buy straightforward fizzy wines such as export Lambrusco in both red and white versions; most are sweet. In general, however, sparkling wines tend to be dry or very dry, though there are a few exceptions to this rule even within Champagne itself. "Brut" and "Extra Brut" indicate dry Champagne and sparkling wines; "Sec", "Demi-Sec" and "Doux" indicate steadily sweeter wines.

Most countries produce inex-

SPARKLING WINES

pensive sparkling wines, often for domestic consumption exclusively: very little Sekt is exported from Germany, for example, and none of Argentina's huge volume of sparkling wine is sent abroad. The two leading exceptions to this rule are Spain's Cava and Australia's inexpensive, branded sparkling wines, both of which have proved popular in other countries. Cava is soft and flowery, with gentle apple notes; Australia's least expensive sparkling wines are more overtly fruity, well-balanced and easy to drink. Yet while the best Cava struggles to approach the quality of good Champagne, Australia's finest sparkling wines can offer great subtlety and finesse, often based (as much Champagne is) on a blend of Pinot Noir and Chardonnay grapes with light lees flavor providing a sense of bready depth. Nonetheless, the best Australian sparkling wines, still have a ripeness and richness to their fruit which distinguishes them from Champagne. Less successful sparkling wines from Australia, as from many warm-climate environments, have an unyielding hardness to them, usually due to fruit being picked before it's ripe to maintain its acidity. Australia also produces some superb red sparkling wines, normally based on Shiraz; these generally require a little more residual sugar than white sparkling wines to balance them, though the wealth of extract and powerful, salty fruit flavor they carry means that the drinker is rarely aware of this. They seem odd at first, but do give them a try: they have unrivaled, fruit-drenched exuberance and vigor, and partner food surprisingly well.

New Zealand, California and South Africa can all produce exciting sparkling wines, with the best from New Zealand and California both showing remarkable complexity and depth of flavor, albeit sometimes combined (especially in New Zealand) with occasional acidic hardness. The most successful sparkling wines of New Zealand and California are those in which the cookie-like, yeasty flavors of a slow second fermentation and extended aging in bottle are most evident, balancing (in California's case) soft summer fruits and (in New Zealand's case) greener citrus fruits.

In Champagne, strangely enough, it can be hard to

discern fruit flavor at all. These are wines grown over an extended season to the barest edge of ripeness; in the base wines from which they are made, very often all the drinker can make out beneath the wincingly acidic sheen is a taut lemony quality. The greatness of Champagne is born out of the fine balance drawn between this tight, almost inarticulate fruit and the subtle yeast flavors the wine acquires as it lies aging beneath the streets of Epernay and Reims. With further storage time (15 years or more), the hidden fruit flavors in the wine seem to emerge into full expression; the wine's color deepens; and it

takes on a wealth of creamy, sometimes even buttery or nutty aromas. To gauge how great Champagne can be, try to cellar some for yourself or taste a well-aged example.

Champagne is available at a range of prices, though it is never inexpensive. The cheapest Champagnes are often green and hard, sometimes with a coarse sugary note, from the *dosage* added before bottling (see page 85); the most expensive Champagnes are almost always very good, but not twice as good as a Champagne at half the price. The best-value Champagnes remain those which bear a vintage date, especially if the

purchaser is able to give them a few years' further cellar storage.

No other European sparkling wine can rival Champagne's depth, intensity and finesse, though one or two can come close. Strangely enough, England's small-scale, northerly vineyards are capable of producing wines of similar balance and poise to Champagne, especially now that Chardonnay and Pinot Noir grapes are being widely cultivated in the chalk and greensand vineyards of Kent and Sussex. Global warming may help England's wine growers shake the certitudes of Champagne still further.

Other French sparkling wines,

sparkling wines

The greatness of Champagne
is born out of
the fine balance drawn between this tight,
almost inarticulate fruit and the
subtle yeast flavors
the wine acquires as it lies aging
beneath the streets of Epernay and Reims.

in particular those of the Loire Valley (Crémant de Loire), Burgundy (Crémant de Bourgogne) and Alsace (Crémant d'Alsace) can all provide complex sparkling wines which, with age, acquire some subtlety. What caps their quality, though, is the fact that making sparkling wine is, for most producers in these regions, a secondary activity; it's what growers use their less-favored vineyard sites for, or what they make with grapes from cooler, wetter years. The result is that many of these wines taste hard, unyielding and sometimes coarse, their flavors betraying unripe fruit.

More interesting in many ways are a number of sparkling wines from little pockets of southern France, often reflecting long and curious local traditions and using regional grape varieties: Clairette or Crémant de Die, Blanquette de Limoux and Gaillac Mousseux. These have soft, textured, summer-fruit flavors, and plenty of yeasty input from the processes of secondary fermentation. Sweet versions also are worth a try.

Germany's sparkling-wine industry has been, in the past, just what that term suggests: large scale, sourcing underripe fruit throughout Europe and turning it into crisp, uncomplicated, often generously sweetened Sekt to be sold at a modest price. Yet Germany's climate is favorable for sparkling wine, and smaller producers have in recent years raised standards greatly. The flavor of a good Riesling-based Sekt remains relatively fruity, though fresh, slender and bracing, too. Sparkling wines are made all over Italy; most common are the low-alcohol, sweet, grapey Moscato versions, at their best in Piedmont's Asti and Alba subregions. Prosecco, a specialty of the Veneto, is a clean, sappy and refreshing fizz.

SWEET WINES

There are two ways of making a wine sweet: the hard way and the easy way. All fully ripe grapes, of course, are packed with sugar; yeasts convert this into alcohol during fermentation. The easy way to make sweet wines is to keep that sugar in its unfermented state, and to give the wine-to-be its necessary preservative strength by adding alcohol from another source. This is called fortification, and we'll take a look at fortified wines later (see page 128).

This section, though, is all about sweet wines which have been made the hard way. Made, in other words, by getting the grapes so ripe and sugar-filled, by various means, that the yeasts eventually give up trying to convert it all into alcohol. What's left in the vat at that stage is a wine of normal strength which still contains plenty of sugar, giving it a sweet flavor. These wines are nearly always risky to make, since you must leave the grapes on the vines later than for most wines. Yields are customarily low, too, so good sweet wine is always expensive. The best, though, provide some of the greatest, most complex and challenging flavors in the wine world.

I mentioned "various means" above; there are three. The first and most widely used is the encouragement of *Botrytis cinerea*, or noble rot. This fungus is a menace when it attacks underripe fruit or red grapes destined to make dry red wine; when it attacks fully ripe, white dessert-wine grapes, however, it acts beneficially, removing water from them, concentrating their sugars and acidity, and providing complex, faintly bitter-edged flavors of its own. The second technique is simply to allow grapes to dry and desiccate on the vine (for which a warm and sunny autumn is essential); and the third approach is to pick perfectly healthy grapes, pack them in slatted wooden trays and store them in warm attics to allow them to dry and desiccate before pressing and fermenting them.

The world's finest sweet wines, it's fair to say, are all created with the help of noble rot; the French, the Germans, the Austrians and the Hungarians are the greatest exponents of this art. Let's begin in France.

Sauternes and Barsac, produced just south of Bordeaux, furnish the world standard for dessert wines: these luscious,

viscous, straw-yellow blends of Sémillon and Sauvignon Blanc slowly deepen to a rich gold with time, acquiring layer after layer of flavor with each passing year. The sweetness of the best Sauternes is never simple: it begins with plenty of fruit flavor behind it (lemon, peach and pineapple are common), and also usually shows the added richness of new oak – a heady combination. The botrytis influence emerges with time (and, in any case, varies from year to year; some Sauternes vintages are made with more desiccated grapes than botrytised ones, while others are totally botrytised). The oak gives the wine a lanolin-like scent and buttery flavor; and the fruits modulate towards a complex, autumn-fruit spectrum. Sauternes proper is generally slightly heavier and richer than the neighboring AOC of Barsac, which often has a deft, lemony elegance. Monbazillac, 100km east of Sauternes on the Dordogne, produces dessert wines of similar style but generally with less complexity; the same is true of lesser Bordeaux sweet-wine appellations like Cérons and Ste Croix du Mont.

France's other great botrytized dessert wines are grown in

Sauternes and Barsac...
furnish the world benchmark
for dessert wines: these
luscious, viscous
straw-yellow blends
of Sémillon and Sauvignon Blanc
slowly deepen
to a rich gold with time,
acquiring layer after layer
of extra flavor with each passing year.

the Loire Valley, in Alsace and in Jurançon. Those of the Loire (sold under a variety of appellations including Vouvray, Montlouis and Bonnezeaux) are made from Chenin Blanc, and usually have a much nervier, edgier balance than rich, fat Sauternes. Flavors include nectarine, peach and apple, and acidity plays an important role in their structure. They age superbly, without losing their pure, limpid, orchardfruit style. With time, the typical Loire Chenin tones of wax, honey and damp straw add complexity.

The dessert wines of Alsace are sold as *vendange tardive* (late harvest) or *sélection des grains nobles* (selection of botrytis-affected grapes), the latter usually being sweeter, richer and more expensive than the former. The exact style of each wine depends on the grape variety from which it is made: Pinot Gris, Gewürztraminer and Riesling are the most common choices. Of the three, Riesling most clearly retains its vivid acidity and mineral notes, backed up by richer citrus-fruit flavors with a pithy, zesty edge. Gewürztraminer should offer its characteristically scented flavors of roses, litchi nuts and soft spices more strongly than usual, while Pinot

Gris is often the richest of all, with sweet, lush, almost tropical-fruit flavors. Both Pinot Gris and Gewürztraminer wines of this level can sometimes seem flaccid because of low acidity.

Despite its position in France's far south, the dessert wines of Jurançon are some of the country's freshest: their high Pyrenean vineyards encourage prominent acidity levels and restrained sweetness, achieved by desiccation rather than botrytis. Dominant fruit flavors include apricot and pineapple, and the tang of botrytis is relatively infrequent.

No other country in the world places more importance on sugar levels in musts than Germany, and almost all of its greatest wines, historically, have been semisweet or fully (sometimes extravagantly) sweet. Every German harvest is a long poker game played by the wine-grower against nature. Depending on weather forecast or intuition, the grower harvests as slowly as possible, leaving the best grapes on the vines until the last moment to achieve maximum ripeness and, with any luck, a dose of botrytis. The result is a hugely nuanced sweetness scale, though in most cases a wine would need to be categorized Auslese, Beerenauslese, Trockenbeerenauslese or Eiswein to qualify as unapologetically sweet.

Auslese wines vary from relatively fresh and delicate in regions such as the Saar, Ruwer or Mosel to decidedly unctuous in more southerly regions such as Pfalz. Wines from the other three categories will all be rich and weighty, including steam-roller-sweet, sugar-saturated Trockenbeerenauslese. Eiswein, however, usually has high acidity levels, giving it a fine-honed edge; many cellar years must pass before this softens. The fundamental difference, yet again, between Germany's sweet wines and those of other countries is the absence of prominent alcohol. Here the game is to paint fruit flavors and aromas into the wines, to allow botrytis to brush depth and complexity onto these, and to balance crystallized fruit sweetness with mouth-freshening acidity. These are, therefore, the least cloying of all dessert wines.

Hungary's great sweet wines, made in the Tokáji region, are the product of a tradition as long-standing and as sophisticated as Germany's. Once again, noble rot is the key, though the Hungarian approach to it is to make an *aszú*, or sweet paste, with all the nobly rotten grapes, which are gathered separately, and then ferment varying proportions of this with dry wines to create medium-sweet or fully sweet wines. The sweet wines of Tokáji are known as Aszú, and the number of *puttonyos* (barrels) of aszú added (three to six) indicates the final sweetness of the wine, with Aszú Eszencia and Eszencia being sweeter still. And the taste? Most Tokáji has a distinct tang to it, from botrytis, from cask maturation and from the wine's natural aging process. Its flavors tend to suggest apricot and apple, dark honey and autumn leaves. It has a finely poised acid balance and a suggestion of minerals; the sweetest examples are thickly textured.

Italy does produce sweet wines based on botrytized fruit, but these are usually the result of individual efforts by the winemaker rather than any long-standing tradition. Sweet wines made from semi-dried or dried grapes are more common. Recioto di Valpolicella, for example, is a sweet red wine produced by drying the grapes after harvest and before vinification: it is strong, with lots of cherry and plum fruit backed by a faint cherry-stone bitterness. Recioto versions of white Soave exist, some of them sparkling, and Tuscany's Vin Santo is also made by the same process of drying white grapes in attics before vinification. Vin Santo varies in quality and style (not all are sweet); many are deliberately oxidized, giving them a sherry-like tang. Sweet versions of white DOC wines such as Orvieto or Albana di Romagna are labeled "Amabile"; these, though, tend to be light and simple in flavor compared with most classic dessert wines.

Southern-hemisphere wine producers have enjoyed the challenge of producing botrytis-affected dessert wines; indeed, Australian and New Zealand winemakers are responsible for the once-obscure term "botrytis-affected" becoming common currency on labels. Botrytis does not develop as regularly in the generally warm, dry and sunny vineyards of the southern hemisphere as in damp and cloudy Europe; it is, therefore, often artificially induced (on varieties such as Semillon, Sauvignon Blanc and Riesling) by producers keen to extend their range of wines. Such sweet wines are often impressive, with massive levels of sweetness, balancing acidity, obvious botrytis flavor and the richness of oak; they are, though, rarely subtle in flavor, and age uncertainly. Much the same can be said of Canada's characterful icewines, made from frozen grapes. The best are dramatic and intense in flavor; less successful examples leave a sweet-and-sour impression in the mouth.

The New World offers fewer examples of sweet wines made by letting grapes dry on the vines, though Klein Constantia in South Africa has recreated the 18th-century legend of Constantia in this way, with impressive results. California's Central Valley has good conditions for this kind of winemaking gambit, too, as Andrew Quady has proved with different styles of sweet Muscat.

A fortified wine is one which has had spirit added to it before, during or after fermentation. That spirit makes further fermentation impossible; any sugar remaining in the wine, therefore, is natural and stable. The spirit also prevents the wine from turning acetic once opened and exposed to the air. You can thus keep bottles of fortified wine open for much longer than ordinary wines, though the spirit doesn't preserve the wine from the effects of oxidation. In most cases (Madeira and Oloroso sherry being the main exceptions), fortified wines are best finished within a week or so of opening.

Historically, they were created to overcome the problems of transporting wine from one country to another by sea in wooden containers. Table wines could easily spoil; fortified wines didn't. As a result, the world's three greatest fortified wines have been drunk and appreciated for hundreds of years in London, Berlin, Stockholm and Savannah.

The first, sherry, comes from mainland Spain; the second, port, from mainland Portugal; and the third from the green Atlantic island called (after the thick forest which originally draped it) *Madeira*, or "wood". We've already explored the different ways in which these wines are made (see "Places", starting page 36); let's look here at their flavors, and the uses to which they are best suited.

Dry Fino sherry is one of the best aperitif wines in the world. Its salty, yeasty, bready flavor has a rigorous, palate-cleansing effect. Manzanilla and Puerto Finos, meanwhile, are softer and saltier. True Amontillado, which should be an aged Fino, shares Fino's delicacy while replacing its supple pungency with dried-apricot fruit and a gentle nuttiness. Palo Cortado (a sherry which began life as a Fino and transmutes later to an Oloroso) adds a little more oxidative bite to this profile.

Oloroso sherry varies from light, tart and slightly varnishy to richly and almost austerely tangy, dry and tongue-scouring, with much higher acidity levels than are found in Fino sherry. Its flavor can be reminiscent of walnuts. Gentle sweetening adds complexity and a balance of flavor to these profiles; clumsy, exaggerated sweetening (as for most "cream" sherries) swamps their fine nuances, making them taste merely raisiny. Pedro Ximénez (PX) sherry, made from sun-dried grapes, is black in color, oily and super-sweet, and tastes like a paste of raisins. It is not dissimilar in style to that other historically distinguished Spanish fortified wine, Málaga, which is dark in color and tastes like the wine equivalent of a rich fruitcake; Cyprus' Commandaria is a further super-sweet, usually fortified wine of knife-and-fork proportions. (Sherry styles, by the way, are duplicated in Montilla-Moriles, though the use of a different base grape variety, Pedro Ximénez, and more restrained fortification tend to give lighter results.)

Like sherry, port can be divided into two broad groups, depending on whether the wine has been aged for some years in a cask or not. Cask-aged ports are called tawnies, and are generally sold with an indication of age (10, 20, 30 or over 40 years old) or in vintage-dated form, as colheita ports. Ironically, the only port sold with the word "Tawny" on its label is in fact an inexpensive blend of young red and white port. True tawnies are relatively delicate wines of a burnished copper color and smooth texture, with intricate flavors of dried fruits, peels and nuts, and even licorice or herbs.

The other branch of the family varies in color from red to black, and is characterized by fresher fruit flavors, more ample tannins, and a vigorous, peppery style. Ruby, vintage character, late-bottled vintage, crusted, quinta vintage and vintage ports all fall into this group, and offer steadily increasing depth and power of flavor. Young vintage port, at the top of the tree, delivers wildly exuberant aromas of crushed red and black fruits and smashed vegetation, explosive tannins, and detonating flavors of plums, cherries, sloes and spices. As ports of this quality age, they calm and settle, acquiring harmony at the same rate as they throw sediment.

Madeira is the world's most oxidized wine style. Indeed, it is not only oxidized but also heat-treated, the combination of the two being what is meant by the word "maderized". This heat-treatment is accomplished artificially (in giant heated vats) for cheap Madeira, and naturally (in sun-lavished attics) for expensive Madeira. There is, sadly, a stark quality difference between the two. Cheap Madeira tastes cooked, confected and sweet, whereas expensive (vintage) Madeira is perhaps the most intense, authoritative and challenging wine in the world, with a fascinating range of aromas and flavors. The exact nature of these depends on the grape variety: dry Sercial can suggest eggs, cheese, straw and furniture polish; medium-dry Verdelho tends to be fruitier, with notes of dessert apple and grape. The sweet Bual can often have a banana sweetness and brown-

FORTIFIED WINES

sugar softness to it, balanced (as always in Madeira) by sustained, fresh acidity, while Malmsey is fruitcake-rich, sometimes with caramel or chocolate notes, too. The casky aromas of all Madeira may suggest, quite literally, the scents of antique stave, but they may also suggest something more ethereal and Cognac-like, which the auctioneer and wine-taster Michael Broadbent compares to crystallized violets.

By comparison with the great Iberian triumvirate, France's contribution to fortified wine culture is modest. Its Muscat *vins doux naturels*, with their grape-sweet scents and luscious flavors, make a delicious drink between (or, if you're French, before) meals; the Moscatel de Valencia of Spain is similar in style and often even better in value. Pineau des Charentes and Floc de Gascogne are both honeyed, lush fortified wines produced by adding Cognac and Armagnac, respectively, to local grape juice (this mixture is known as a *mistelle* or, officially, *vin de liqueur*). France's most ambitious fortified wines, however, are the red and white wines of Banyuls and Rivesaltes, near the Spanish border; red versions of these can resemble light port, with lots of cherry fruit, deft tannins, tangy oxidation (especially in *rancio* versions) and licorice spice.

Italy's most notable fortified wine is one which, like Spain's Málaga, has fallen on hard times of late: Marsala. Cheap versions are caramelly and confected; the best dry Marsala, though, is a pale, soft-textured, almost buttery wine of impressive style. Good dry Marsala is, like olive oil, known as "virgin" (*vergine*). Greece has the dark red, pruney Mavrodaphne of Patras to offer fortified-wine lovers; this tastes like a well-bolstered Recioto. Some of Samos' famous Muscat wines are fortified (Anthemis), while others are merely rich dessert wines (Nektar).

The two southern-hemisphere countries with the longest traditions of fortified winemaking are South Africa and Australia. Both produce accomplished port-style and sherry-style wines, though the demand for the latter has dwindled considerably in recent years, and it is doubtful these will survive. South Africa's port-style wines (including some based on Portuguese grape varieties like Tinta Barroca) are lush and jammy; Australia's versions are denser and sturdier. Australia (particularly the Rutherglen region of Victoria) produces an outstanding range of fortified Liqueur Muscat and Liqueur Tokay (ie Muscadelle) wines, too: these are sweet, thick and syrupy, yet their long cask-aging lends them a carefully integrated oxidative complexity. Hidden within the intense sweetness, you'll find flavors of rose, walnut, caramel and chocolate.

Most of this book is, as its title suggests, written to help you chart the delicious multiplicity of tastes and styles offered by wine. In conclusion, let's examine a few practicalities which will help you enjoy your wines as fully as possible.

the pleasure of wine

BUYING WINE

The strict laws governing the sale of alcohol in some states of the US make the business of choosing and buying wine "easy" – there is no real choice, as the local government controls where and what you can buy. In the other "free-market" states, though, where is the best place to buy wine? That depends on the type of wine you enjoy drinking, and the amount of money you have to spend on it. Supermarkets, discount warehouses, and superstores are usually the cheapest source of all and should provide a large selection of wines suitable for everyday drinking. Such operations, however, need container-loads of a wine simply to be able to offer it through-out all their chains; so they tend to favor bigger producers and heavily promoted wine brands over more interesting wines produced on a small scale by enterprising winemakers.

For those more complex bottles which, for true enthusiasts, lie at the heart of wine's appeal, you will generally need to browse through the list or the shelves of an independent wine specialty shop, as it is here that almost all the most interesting tastes and styles are likely to be found. You may have to spend a little more than in a supermarket or discount store, but the wines will repay this in extra depth and flavor.

Finding the finest wines of all can be extremely difficult, even though their high prices might seem dissuasive. For a start, they are usually made in relatively small quantities, and there are more than enough wine-lovers to quickly snap up supplies. Fine wine stores usually stock such wines for a short period when they are first released; supplies are quickly exhausted, and the wines are cellared until maturity by private collectors. To buy mature examples of classic wines, you'll need to use auction houses or reputable wine merchants.

If we **love** wine,
it is because it offers us
something of
nature's diversity
to enjoy intimately,
in scent and in flavor,
at the same time as its alcohol
soothes our spirits.

STORING WINE

Once bought, where do you put your wine? Wine needs darkness (readily achievable by covering racks or bottles with blankets); a steady, coolish temperature; and a lack of vibration. A cellar or basement – dark, humid, constantly cool – is ideal, but few modern houses, and not all older houses, have one. If you don't have a cellar, the best place for your wine is a darkish closet towards the center of the house, or perhaps underneath a seldom-used spare bed. Avoid attics and garages, since their wide temperature fluctuations will prematurely age wine; for the same reason kitchens are unsuitable. If you have less-than-perfect storage facilities, keep wine at home for a few months at most, and invest in professional storage for wines which need years to evolve. Many wine stores offer customers cellaring facilities.

SERVING

Glassware is a subjective matter, yet it is startlingly true that wines actually smell and taste better from some glasses than from others. The ideal shape for a glass is tulip-like, with the rim smaller in diameter than the widest point of the bowl: this helps concentrate the wine's aroma. Thin, uncut glass is better for enjoying and gauging the color of a wine than thick, cut glass; and larger glasses are infinitely preferable to smaller ones. To enjoy a wine's aroma, a glass needs to be no more than half-full, and in a small glass such a serving seems mean. Champagne and sparkling wines are best served in a tall, elegant tulip, ideally with the inner base of the bowl terminating in a point: this displays the stream of bubbles to best effect. However, even the smallest trace of detergent residue can flatten the fizz, so take extra care to rinse the glasses well in hot water after washing, and dry them thoroughly with a linen cloth while they are still warm.

The serving temperature of wine is worth a little thought and planning. The key point to remember is that the tag "white wine chilled, red wine at room temperature" is actually too imprecise a rule of thumb to do wine justice. Most refrigerators are kept at 39° or 41°F – too cold for all but sweet or sparkling wine. White wines in general are best served at 46°F or so, and richer dry white wines (like white burgundy) at 51° or 54°F. Light red wines, by contrast, often need chilling: reds from the Loire and Beaujolais are ideal at 57°F, and even the best red burgundy or Pinot Noir should not be served at much more than 61°F. The biggest red wines are ideal at a maximum of 64° or 66°F which means that serving red wine at "room temperature" on a warm summer's day is to serve it too hot. Use your refrigerator intelligently by getting deeply chilled white wines out of it a little while before you need them, and putting red wines into it for a gentle chill where appropriate, particularly on the hottest days of summer.

The custom of opening wine for an hour or so before you serve it to "let it breathe" is a waste of time, since far too little of the wine is exposed to air for it to make any difference. There is a sound principle at work, though, which is that oxygenation helps young wines to open up and gain the articulacy which might otherwise come only with age. The best way to give them this is to decant them – or, if you don't have a decanter, to pour the wines out into a jug, rinse the bottle, and then pour them back into the bottle. Do this for any top-quality

red or white wine which you're serving during the first quarter of its estimated life span; indeed, almost all youngish reds will be improved by this treatment, regardless of their quality.

Decanting to separate a wine (or port) from its sediment is a different matter altogether. In this case, you will probably be about to drink a fully mature or even old wine. The oxygenation which comes from decanting can sometimes freshen such wines, but it can also lead to rapid collapse in the truly senile, so decant with care. With red burgundy of advanced years it is generally better to accept that the last glass or two may contain some sediment than to rattle its old and frail bones about in a decanter.

WINE FAULTS

What if, horrible to contemplate, the wine you have bought, cellared and finally opened for a big event proves to be disgusting? There is, unfortunately, nothing to be done in such cases except to put it aside to return to its source and to open another one. It's important to know, however, if there is actually something wrong with it (a wine fault) or if it is simply over-aged or in some other way not to your taste.

The most common wine fault at present is corkiness. This does not mean that there are pieces of cork floating about in the wine; rather, it refers to an unpleasant taint which corks infected with a compound called 2,4,6- trichloranisole leave in the scent and flavor of a wine. Corked wines smell musty, like damp cardboard; their true flavors become subsumed in this chemical decay, for which there is no remedy.

The next most common wine fault is sulfur spoilage. This comes in two forms. The first, most frequent in young German wines, is an excess of free sulfur: you are likely to feel this as a shock to the nose and lungs rather than smell it; it can even provoke asthma attacks. Decant the wine a couple of times, and it generally dissipates.

In mature wines, the sulfur binds with other compounds to form sulfide smells. At low levels, these may even add a leathery or farmyardy complexity to a wine; at higher levels, they make it stink of eggs, socks, manure or substances still less appetizing. Decanting may help; you could also try dropping a copper coin into the wine.

Oxidation is another wine fault, though relatively uncommon today in internationally traded wines. Oxidized wines smell and taste flat, stale, tired and dull, and their color is likely to be yellower or browner than it should be. Wines are occasionally spoiled, too, by excess volatile acidity, detectable as a sharp, solvent-like smell.

If a wine is hazy, or if it's sparkling when it should be still, then there is something wrong with it, too. Do remember, though, that many white wines are bottled with a generous dose of dissolved CO_2 to keep them fresh, so a little prickle of gas in a newly opened white is generally not a fault. If a wine smells and tastes clean, then it is sound; unwanted refermentations will always be accompanied by unpleasant or disconcerting smells and flavors.

Sediment is nearly always good news for the consumer, meaning that a wine has not been excessively filtered or fined before bottling. This is as true for white wines as for

red. If you find tiny crystals attached to the cork of a wine, or floating about in it as a sediment, don't worry; these are perfectly harmless tartrates and, once again, this is a sign that a wine has not been excessively processed before bottling. Indeed, I am disappointed in, and suspicious of, any top-quality still wine which does not throw some sort of a sediment after a few years' storage; it should be there.

CHOOSING WINE IN RESTAURANTS

Buying wine in a restaurant presents special challenges. The first is coping with the cost of what you are offered, usually twice or three times the wine's retail price, even though the restaurateur has probably bought the wine more cheaply than you can. The result is that most restaurant drinkers are limited to choosing from among the half-dozen cheapest wines on the list, unless (fortunately) a rich friend or a company is paying for the meal, or (commendably) the restaurant in question offers a range of wines by the glass. Another challenge is that those sharing a meal will probably be eating a variety of dishes, which rarely happens at home. The

third and final challenge is that all the listed wines may be completely new to you.

Wine waiters should, of course, be friendly, helpful and truthful; most now are. The best solution to choosing wine well in a restaurant is to talk to the wine waiter about the choices open to you and judge the restaurant according to the success (or otherwise), of the recommendations that follow your discussion.

If you're not in the mood for that, try to choose wines which are consistent in quality and amenable with a variety of foods; whites from the Loire, light reds from Beaujolais, and many New World wines make relatively inexpensive, successful restaurant choices. If you recognize that a wine is faulty (corkiness is all too common), point this out to the wine waiter and offer it for his inspection; the bottle should be replaced free of charge. Badly made wines, by contrast, must be endured, but don't hurry back to a restaurant which lists them.

WINE AND FOOD

Time for food, finally. There are two schools of thought on food and wine matches. One school, which we might call the legislators, holds that there are perfect wine matches

It is **startlingly true** that wines actually **smell** and **taste better** from **some glasses** than from others.

for every dish and probably perfect dishes for every wine. The other school, the anarchists, maintains that since no dish is ever prepared the same way twice, since no two bottles ever taste the same, and since flavors and combinations are affected by the drinker's mood, the weather and probably the phases of the moon, any assertion of ideal combinations is doomed to failure. You might as well eat what you want and drink what you fancy, throwing the two together with a little common sense; as often as not, the combination will work out.

Both points of view have their merits, and temperamentally I'm more inclined to anarchy in this matter than to legislation. All the same, great bottles of wine can be squandered by partnering them with the wrong foods, so giving a little thought in advance to combinations is worthwhile. Here is a rough guide to happy matches.

Red meat and red wine have had a love affair for thousands of years; you can't go seriously wrong, but try to match the biggest, beefiest reds with stews, casseroles and fatty meats, while the lighter, finer, more graceful reds are best with plain, lean meats. White meats like chicken, pork and rabbit go well with almost any wine, red or white; middleweight reds and rich whites are particularly suitable. Fattier poultry dishes, such as those based on duck or goose, are good with reds which contain both high tannin levels and plenty of acidity (time to roll out your Barolo); they also partner acidic, masterful whites like Loire Valley whites based on Chenin Blanc, or Riesling from almost anywhere.

Fish, needless to say, goes well with white wine – yet it can go well with red wine, too. Light, chilled red wine with roast cod, for example, is an excellent combination. An oilier, richer fish like salmon or

mackerel generally needs white wine. Chablis and Sancerre are the classic partners, but most Chardonnay is supremely amenable to fish, while New Zealand Sauvignon Blanc or Australian Riesling make more adventurous, boisterous choices. Seafood tends to need dry, taut whites such as Muscadet or (a personal favorite) well-chilled dry Fino or Manzanilla sherry.

Vegetarian dishes are good with softish reds from countries like Chile, Argentina or South Africa; salads respond well to the bright and positive flavors of New World whites in general (though go easy on the dressing if you want to avoid upsetting the wine). Spicy foods from the Indian or Thai traditions need either very soft reds (Chile again) or gentle whites (from Italy, for example, or parts of the French countryside like Bergerac or Gaillac). The touch of sweetness offered by, say, an Alsace Gewürztraminer or Muscat can also enhance subtly spicy flavors.

Cheese, contrary to popular belief, is actually quite difficult to match with wine; sweet and fortified wines are best. "Dessert" wines, too, don't always marry contentedly with dessert; in general, sweet fortified wines have more punch and push to them, and make a better match. A great dessert wine, in my opinion, should be served in place of, rather than with, dessert, perhaps accompanied by a little plain cheese and some oat biscuits.

Have fun, experiment, explore: what's true for food-and-wine matching is true for the discovery of wine itself. Anyone with an eye for nature will know that diversity is beauty. If we love wine, it is because it offers us something of nature's diversity to enjoy intimately, in scent and in flavor, at the same time as its alcohol soothes our spirits. I wish you much pleasure in wine.

INDEX

Page numbers in **bold** refer to main entries

index

Bibliography

The following four books provide a fine foundation for a wine library.

The Story of Wine, Hugh Johnson
(Mitchell Beazley)
The World Atlas of Wine, Hugh Johnson
(Simon & Schuster)
Parker's Wine Buyer's Guide, Robert Parker
(Fireside)
The Oxford Companion to Wine, ed Jancis
Robinson (Oxford University Press)

Should you wish to find out more about particular regions, there are usually specialty reference guidebooks available for these. Here are some of the best, together with other stimulating general wine reference books.

The Wine Atlas of Italy, Burton Anderson
(Mitchell Beazley)
Barolo to Valpolicella: The Wines of Northern Italy, Nicolas Belfrage (Faber & Faber)
The Wines of California, Stephen Brook
(Faber & Faber)
Oz Clarke's Wine Atlas, Oz Clarke
(Little, Brown)
Côte d'Or: A Celebration of Great Wines of Burgundy, Clive Coates M. W. (University California Press)
Grands Vins: The Finest Châteaux of Bordeaux and Their Wines, Clive Coates M. W. (University California Press)
The Bordeaux Atlas and Encyclopaedia of Châteaux, Hubrecht Duijker (St. Martins Press)
French Country Wines, Rosemary George
(Faber & Faber)
The Wines of New Zealand, Rosemary George
(Faber & Faber)
The Art & Science of Wine, James Halliday and Hugh Johnson (Simon & Schuster)
Wine Atlas of Australia and New Zealand, James Halliday (HarperCollins Australia)
Burgundy, Anthony Hanson (Faber & Faber)
Madeira, Alex Liddell (Faber & Faber)

The Wines of the Rhône, John Livingstone-Learmonth (Faber & Faber)
The Wild Bunch: Great Wines from Small Producers, Patrick Matthews (Faber & Faber)
Rhône Renaissance, Remington Norman (Wine Appreciation Guild)
Bordeaux: A Comprehensive Guide to the Wines Produced from 1961 to 1997, Robert Parker
(Simon & Schuster)
The Wine Atlas of Germany: and Traveler's Guide to the Vineyards, Stuart Pigott
(Mitchell Beazley)
South African Wines, John Platter
(Platter Wine Guide SA)
The New Spain, John Radford
(Mitchell Beazley)
The Wines of Alsace, Tom Stevenson
(Faber & Faber)
World Encyclopedia of Champagne and Sparkling Wines, Tom Stevenson (Wine Appreciation Guild)
The Wine Atlas of California and the Pacific Northwest; A Traveler's Guide to the Vineyards, Bob Thompson (Simon & Schuster)
Terroir, James E. Wilson (University California Press)

Acknowledgments

We would like to thank the following companies for allowing us to photograph their vineyards, wineries, and cellars.

CALIFORNIA
Beringer Wine Estates, St Helena, Napa Valley
Schramsberg Vineyards, Napa Valley
Heitz Wine Cellars, St Helena, Napa Valley
De Loach Vineyards, Sonoma Valley
Iron Horse Vineyards, Sonoma Valley

AUSTRALIA
Rockford Vineyards, Barossa Valley, South Australia
Henschke, Barossa Valley, South Australia
Peter Lehmann, Barossa Valley, South Australia
d'Arenberg, McLaren Vale, South Australia
Leeuwin Estate, Margaret River, Western Australia

SPAIN
Bodegas Muga, Haro
La Rioja Alta, Haro

FRANCE
Château Margaux, Pauillac
Château Canon, St Emilion
Château Belair, St Emilion
Château Latour, Pauillac

We would also like to thank the following companies and establishments for their help.

Maison des Vins, St Emilion
Andrew and Jo Davies at D'Arrys Verandah Restaurant, McLaren Vale, South Australia
AP Johns Cooperage, Tenunda, NSW
Mark and Joanne McNamara, Pear Tree Cottage Restaurant, Greenock, NSW
Mark Neal, Jack Neal & Son, Napa Valley